UNIVERSITY LIBRARY
UW-STEVENS POINT

Vote Power

SALE PRICE
25 ¢

VOTE POWER

THE
OFFICIAL
ACTIVIST
CAMPAIGNER'S
HANDBOOK

by the MOVEMENT FOR A NEW CONGRESS

Prentice-Hall, Inc.,
Englewood Cliffs, N.J.

This handbook was prepared by Edward Schneier and William T. Murphy, Jr., with the assistance of Henry Beinen, Leigh H. Beinen, Bruce B. Blackadar, Michael Cohen, Robert K. Durkee, Fred Goldrich, Nancy Lambert, Janice B. Schneier, and the staff of the National Office of the Movement for a New Congress.

We wish gratefully to acknowledge the comments and suggestions of Richard E. Ayres, The Vera Foundation; James David Barber, Yale University; Stephen Golden, Columbia University; Stanley Kelley, Jr., Princeton University; Michael Rappaport, Opinion Research Corporation; and Matthew A. Reese, Matthew Reese Associates.

© 1970 by The Movement for a New Congress (Palmer Hall, Princeton, N.J.)

All rights reserved. No part of this book may be reproduced in any form or by any means without permission in writing from the publisher.

P 13-944140-9
C 13-944157-3

Library of Congress Catalog Card Number 77-131944

Printed in the United States of America

Current printing (last number): 10 9 8 7 6 5 4 3 2 1

JK
2283
.M68

Contents

306008

Resource Materials 53

Preface

Millions of Americans are working for peace. Most of them are ineffective. In politics, sincerity, dedication, and good will are not enough. No prizes are given for running second in an election or for being a nice guy. If nice guys are to win elections--and winning is the name of the game--they must know what they are doing, why they are doing it, and how they can work most effectively to maximize electoral support.

This book tells the average citizen how he can most effectively participate in the political process. It is both a how-to-do-it manual and a book that explains why some techniques are better than others. It is a citizen's guide to the art of political victory.

Vote Power was prepared by the National Office of the Movement for a New Congress, a campus-based movement operating within the American political tradition to mobilize massive grass-roots volunteer efforts to elect a new Congress. The Movement's purpose is to reorder national priorities through direct participation in crucial Congressional campaigns.

This handbook, although intended primarily for those who share our commitments to the causes of peace, racial justice, and the reordering of national priorities, should prove equally useful to all citizens, regardless of political persuasion, who wish to be more effective politically. Though aimed particularly at the 1970 Congressional campaign, the general principles, proposals, and techniques described here should prove applicable to all campaigns, at all levels, for many years to come.

Every candidate will have his own ideas about the best ways of arranging the technical details of his campaign. It is not our purpose in this book to debate the relative merits of 3-by-5 as opposed to 4-by-7 cards. What we have tried to do is explain in general terms the ways in which volunteers can maximize their impact on the political process. Thus Chapter 1 emphasizes the importance of selectivity, of focusing energies on those campaigns which are most likely to succeed. We would stress in particular the channeling of volunteers into the 119 most marginal House districts listed in Part A of the Resource Materials at the end of the book.

Chapter 2 is a brief description of one of the campaigns in which student activists have already been involved: the unsuccessful primary race of Lew Kaden in New Jersey. The purpose of this chapter is both to describe in general terms the ways in which student volunteers can have an impact and to point up some of the pitfalls of bad planning in a campaign of this kind. Chapters 3, 4, and 5 are concerned with the specific services volunteers can perform, from registration drives and canvassing to research and polling. These chapters combine detailed descriptions of how to do it with analyses of the reasons for preferring certain techniques to others.

Finally, in Chapter 6 we offer some suggestions for following through on the efforts launched this fall: how to keep tabs on your Representative in Congress and make him a more effective Congressman, how to continue to be an active force in the American political process. Appendix B provides a specially prepared compilition of the voting records of all incumbent Senators and Representatives in 1968, 1969, and the first six months of 1970.

People will vote for a candidate for many reasons--they like his stands on the issues, the way he combs his hair, they are distantly related to his brother-in-law's second cousin--but the most compelling reason of all is simply that somebody whose opinions they respect asked them to. There is no substitute for face-to-face contact with the voters. And there is no substitute for active volunteers who are informed, articulate, and who know what they are doing.

Whatever the social goals that motivate people to go into politics, the best way to achieve those goals is to elect candidates who share them. Some politicians are shrewd. Some are obtuse. All know how to count votes. Nothing could be more important to the future of American society than the way in which those votes are distributed on the first Tuesday of November. On election night they don't count the issues, they count votes.

1
Working Toward
a New Congress

Seldom has American history seen such widespread discontent with our governmental institutions, with the tone and direction of public policies, and with the state of our politics. Especially among minorities-- nonwhites, the young, the poor--there is a strong and growing dissatisfaction with the institutions of American politics. The gap between the traditional ideals and expectations of these groups, on one hand, and the realities of contemporary politics, on the other, is nowhere more evident than in the Halls of Congress. The House of Representatives particularly has shown a clear and deep-seated reluctance to confront the problems of war, racism, and misdirected priorities. In that body the frustrations of liberals run deepest, fear of reform is greatest, and the forces of reaction are strongest. It is in the House that pollution control, education, and poverty funds are cut; that Mitchell, Agnew, and the Ohio National Guard are applauded; that arms budgets are never cut; that congressional reform bills languish; and that foreign aid bills are amended to send planes to Chiang Kai-shek.

WHAT POWERS DOES CONGRESS HAVE?

To describe this era as one of Executive force is commonplace. In both foreign and domestic policies, the Executive branch has become, in Richard Neustadt's words, "the regular, accustomed source of all major initiatives." Yet the Congress of the United States remains the strongest legislative body in the world. Its potential powers are vast. An assertive, bold, and dynamic Congress, one that both checks and activates the Executive, one that both responds to an anticipates social change, is essential to the future health and welfare of our society.

The 91st Congress, particularly the Senate, has given encouraging signs that the legislative branch of the federal government is moving toward a reassertion of its constitutional role in the area of foreign policy and toward a reaffirmation of its responsibility for ordering domestic priorities. The repeal of the Gulf of Tonkin resolution, the adoption of the Cooper-Church amendment on Cambodia, the rejections of Haynesworth and Carswell, and the votes to override presidential vetoes of bills appropriating money for health care and education are encouraging signs. They must be sanctioned and reinforced by the electorate.

1

WHAT ARE THE STAKES IN THE 1970 ELECTIONS?

A fine and delicate balance exists between progressive and reactionary forces in the 91st Congress. In the House a shift of 25 to 30 seats would have a profound impact on public policy. In the Senate the stakes of the 1970 elections are unusually high. That third of the Senate which faces reelection this year was originally elected in the recession year of 1958. It was reelected during the Johnson landslide of 1964. The result, as Senator George McGovern has pointed out, is that

> more than half of the liberals in the United States Senate are up
> for reelection in 1970, and fewer than a fifth of the conservatives.
> There is a statistically unusual but nonetheless imminent threat that
> the election could leave the liberals substantially weaker in the
> Senate than at any time since the early 1950's--and possibly even the
> 1920's... And even losses as moderate as those of last year would
> permit the Republicans to organize the Senate and give conservatives
> of both parties a commanding long-term majority. Not the least of
> the stakes will be the ability of surviving Democrats to keep the
> chairmanships of committees and subcommittees in such vital areas as
> foreign relations, education, civil rights, poverty, hunger, conser-
> vation, pollution, tax reform, consumer protection, and urban re-
> development.

Consider some specific issues in the 91st Congress. The addition of two doves in the Senate would have defeated the ABM; the loss of five liberal seats would have tipped the balance in favor of both Haynesworth and Carswell; three new liberals could have saved the legal services projects of the Office of Economic Opportunity.

Prowar margins have been greater on foreign-policy issues in the House than in the Senate. The domestic balance, however, has been very close. Thus, the administration's "Southern Strategy" substitute for the Voting Rights Act of 1970 passed by only five votes. A four-vote conservative margin saved Nixon's veto of the HEW appropriations.

At stake in 1970 are 435 seats in the House and 35 in the Senate. At stake too is the tone of our politics for the next two years. Rightly or not, the 1970 elections will be widely interpreted as a barometer of the national mood. Just as the 1968 election returns were used to vindicate the Southern Strategy, so will the Congressional campaign of 1970 be used to gauge the strength of the "silent majority." Should the forces of reaction hold their own in 1970, the voices of Agnew and Mitchell will be strengthened in the inner councils of the administration. Should outspoken Congressional doves go down to defeat, less bold liberals will retreat to safer pastures.

Party leadership is also at issue in this election. Will conservative Republicans in the Senate be able to replace Minority Leader Hugh Scott with Roman Hruska? Who will replace the retiring John McCormack as Speaker of the House? What about reforms in the seniority system that the House Democratic caucus voted to take up next January? And, of course, who will emerge from the 1970 elections as likely candidates for the Presidency in 1972?

WHAT STANDS IN THE WAY OF CHANGE?

The answers to some of these questions will be slow to emerge. The Congress that convenes in January 1971 will probably not be radically different from the one that sits in Washington now. Barring plague, natural catastrophe, or a rash of unexpected resignations, about two-thirds of the Senate's 100 members will return automatically. A very high percentage of the 435 members of the House of Representatives will be returned almost as easily. A basic fact of American politics is that most seats in Congress are safe for the incumbents. Typically, we can expect 38 of 535 Senators and Representatives to resign or retire during a two-year session; 13 will die; 11 will be defeated in a party primary; and 31 will lose their seats in the November election. Fewer than 100, in other words, or about 17% will fail to be reelected--only about half of those because of defeat at the polls. In the context of recent political history, a shift of more than 30 seats in the November elections must be considered a landslide.[1]

Strength of the Incumbent The advantages of incumbency are termendous. Unlike many of their challengers, incumbent Senators and Representatives are experienced campaigners. For at least two years they have been able to perform countless services for their constituents. They have been invited to give scores of commencement addresses, present plaques to Boy Scout heroes, cut ribbons opening new stores, factories, and highways. Their names are constantly in the press. Their staffs in Washington spend much of their time cultivating constituents. They have the use of the franking privilege whereby their mailings, unlike those of their challengers, are delivered free of charge. Those who identify with the Nixon administration, moreover, have the added advantage of White House favors, campaign appearances, and funds.[2]

Off-year Voters A second problem of New Congress candidates in 1970 is that the off-year electorate tends to have a strong upper-class and conservative bias. The young and the poor generally have poor voting records as compared with older, more affluent citizens. These differences are even more marked in nonpresidential years, when only the best-informed and most highly motivated are likely to vote.[3]

Money The third problem is money. Big money in the United States is often used to buy political access. As a rule it goes to those who are already in power. The administration in power has a much greater ability than the out-party to attract campaign contributions. Witness the contrast between 1964, when the incumbent Democrats received 69% of their $25 million campaign kitty in amounts of more than $500, and 1968, when Hubert Humphrey's losing campaign ended in a still-unpaid deficit of close to $8 million. Spiro Agnew alone, it has been estimated, will raise close to $8 million for 1970 Republican Congressional candidates (who are already solvent). Most of this money will go to candidates who are committed to the war and to continuation of business-as-usual at home.[4]

Apathy A final barrier to the election of a new Congress is the reluctance of many citizens to become actively involved in the political process. People who are committed to changing the system are not always prepared to act on the basis of that commitment. Reformers, Boss Plunkett of Tammany Hall observed at the turn of the century, are "mornin' glories--looked lovely in the mornin' and withered up in a short time, while the

regular machines went on flourishin' forever, like fine old oaks." Not
all reformers are political morning glories (nor are too many of those
fine old oaks still flourishing), but the description comes uncomfortably
close to the mark. Campaigning is hard work, and the rewards for volunteers are at best intangible.

The first rule of volunteer politics is simple: Don't get discouraged.
Don't get discouraged if doors are slammed in your face; it happens all
the time. Don't get discouraged by the mountains of donkey work that must
be done; think what it would cost to hire professional stamp-lickers.
Don't get discouraged if your candidate picks his nose; his opponent does,
too.

WHAT ARE THE OPPORTUNITIES FOR WINNING?

Some of the best candidates running in 1970 will go down to igno-
minious defeat. Some of the worst will win handily. Millions of Americans support the war in Vietnam. The white backlash is not a myth.
Neither is the backlash against campus protest. But the opportunities
for electing a more responsible Congress are good for a least three
reasons.

The Out-Party in the Off-Year. The party in power tends naturally
to lose seats in an off-year election. Supporters of the Nixon administration, whether they like it or not, must run on its record. That
record includes:

High unemployment
Continued inflation
Cutbacks in housing, health, and education
Continuation of the war

Although it would be folly to underestimate Nixon's appeal to the "silent
majority," the tendency of the American voter is to vote against those
policies he dislikes rather than for those he likes.

Low Turnout A second important factor in 1970 is low voter turnout.
Low turnout, as pointed out, tends to favor conservatives. Massive volunteer efforts, however, can reverse this trend. The major effect of
door-to-door canvassing, as we shall see in Chapter 4, is to increase
turnout. Thus, in an off-year, selective canvassing activities--aimed
only at neighborhood with a high potential for supporting your candi-
date--are less likely to be offset by other appeals.

A district that in 1968 elected a hawkish Democrat by a margin of
85,000 to 75,000 might be expected in 1970 to reelect him by a margin of
58,000 to 50,000. Through selective canvassing and election-day activities however, an attractive Republican candidate might be able to mobilize the necessary 10,000 stay-at-home Republicans needed to turn the
election around.

Voting by Party The Democrats should be the big gainers in 1970.
The natural tendency of the party in power to lose seats in an off-year
will be compounded in 1970 by a second characteristic of the off-year
electorate: its tendency to vote party. A 1958 poll by the Survey Research Center of the University of Michigan showed that an "astonishingly
small proportion of the mid-term vote is cast by political Independents."
Moreover, "something like 84% of all the votes for the House in 1958 were

4

cast by party identifiers supporting their parties."[4] In 1970, in other words, we can expect that the Independents who voted for Nixon and Wallace in 1968 will not vote in 1970. The party identifiers, who remain overwhelmingly Democratic, will return to the fold in 1970. Since the voting records presented in the Appendix to this book show that Democrats tend generally to be more dovish and liberal than Republicans, this factor--with a few notable exceptions--should help to bring the ideal of a New Congress closer to reality.

Activism   Perhaps the most important reason for cautious optimism in 1970 is the enthusiasm of thousands of volunteer activists for meaningful action designed to change the system. Spawned by President Nixon's April 30 announcement of American involvement in Cambodia, fed by the killings at Kent State and Jackson State, and buoyed by memories of 1968, when student political power hastened the retirement of President Johnson, dozens of new organizations have been created to channel these energies. Students and faculty members at Dartmouth created the Continuing Presence in Washington to activate and coordinate citizens' lobbying efforts on behalf of antiwar proposals. The Universities National Anti-War Fund in one month raised more than $50,000 for Congressional peace candidates.

The Movement   The idea of focusing student energies on Congressional campaigns was developed through the Movement for a New Congress at Princeton University. The MNC was organized on the assumption that students could be organized to alter the composition of Comgress by changing the balance of power in House and Senate races in highly competitive districts.

A series of lobbying and fund-raising groups has sprouted on campuses in the wake of the Cambodian invasion--but the Movement was the only large-scale effort to direct student protest into electoral politics and to transform the Congressional elections through massive person-to-person campaigns. The Movement has contacted over 600 colleges, and more than 400 of these are currently serving as local chapters. Local chapters are coordinated within each region by a regional center (regions are roughly equivalent to states). Five regional centers are currently functioning.

Two Weeks for Peace   One idea that has caught on around the country and is strongly supported by MNC would free students and faculty members from academic obligations for two weeks just before Election Day. This idea was first suggested at Princeton in early May. Students asked for a pre-election recess so that those who wanted to become actively involved in campaigns would not miss class work. The Princeton faculty voted to begin the academic year a week early, eliminate Thanksgiving recess, and delay the Christmas holiday in order to establish a two-week recess immediately preceding November 3.

As of early July, 18 other colleges had adopted a similar calendar adjustment to enable students to work for political candidates during the fall. It is highly probable that at least a dozen additional colleges will adopt the idea, and many other schools are considering either this plan or some alternative. Some local chapters are working this summer to persuade their schools to adopt such a recess.

THE HARD REALITIES OF EFFECTIVE ACTION

Winning elections is more than just hard work. Success in politics requires skill, dedication, and a willingness to work with what you've got.

No one has ever been able scientifically to identify the forces that combine to produce a successful politician. Why was Dwight Eisenhower a winner and Adlai Stevenson a loser? What strange combination of circumstances elevated Spiro Agnew to his lofty post in our system? These are fascinating questions for a seminar in American government. They are deadly traps to the amateur politician. The fact is that for 1970 at least, we are stuck with what we have.

Some unappealing men in Congress vote right. Some very appealing candidates for public office vote wrong 98% of the time. Here, then, is Rule 2 of practical politics: Keep your eye upon the donut and not upon the hole. Remember that there is no perfect candidate, no Lochinvar on a white steed who has the perfect solution to each and every one of the nation's problems. We are moreover, too late to choose our own candidates; we have to run with the horses that are already on the track.

Remember above all that winning is the name of the game. To win, a candidate must appeal not just to you but to 40,000 to 100,000 other voters. The composition of the district may dictate a campaign based on economic issues rather than on the war. It may call for emphasizing a very narrow set of local issues, such as help for the fishing industry or opposition to government plans to close down a veterans' hospital. If issues such as these can win votes for your candidate, these are the issues that should be pushed. As campaign consultant Matthew A. Reese says, "To win, you don't talk with a guy who has lost his job about the development of the foreign policy which led to Vietnam--even if, by chance, you understand it.... Fit the issue to the voter."

Simple as this sounds, it is difficult in practice. Most of us will work in this campaign because we feel very strongly about certain issues, the war in particular. But those who want to be active in politics so they can talk about the war can throw this book away. That is not what political campaigns are all about. Stephen Shadegg, who engineered Barry Goldwater's initial upset campaign for the Senate, argues:

> Voters don't elect philosophers to public office, they elect candidates. Approached in the right fashion at the right time, a voter can be persuaded to give his ballot to a candidate whose philosophy is opposed to the cherished notions of the voter.[6]

Perhaps this is too cynical and hard-nosed. It may also be true. Keeping your eye upon the donut means remembering at all times that one new vote in Congress against the ABM is worth far more than one or two browbeaten converts in a door-to-door canvass. Again, the basic point: election boards count votes, not issues.

Who Needs Help? Counting both House and Senate, there will be 470 congressional elections in 1970. Close to 1,000 candidates of both parties will be seeking volunteer campaign help. Most of them will get far less than they need. Many, however, will get more help than they deserve.

Given limited resources, effective political action must be selective political action. When you're hunting ducks, you go where the ducks are. Similarly, when your goal is the election of a new Congress, you go where you have a reasonable chance of winning. In Appendix A we have listed the nation's 100 most marginal Congressional districts; these are the districts to focus attention on this fall. The choice, as Matthew Reese puts it, is between enjoying "the excitement and publicity of reducing the victory margin of a hawk you cannot possibly beat," or using "the same manpower and time to elect several peace candidates in less glamorous marginal districts."[7]

Between 1952 and 1968, 785 seats in the House of Representatives (20.1%) were won by candidates who received less than 55% of the two-party vote. Of those who ran again in the following election, 125 (17.5%) were defeated. Of the more than 3,000 incumbents who had received more than 55%, only 4.5% were defeated in the next election. Not a single one of the candidates receiving more than 65% of the two-party vote in 1966 were defeated in 1968.

It is highly unlikely that any such upsets will be scored this year either. It would be nice to beat Mendell Rivers. It would delight many of us to see William Jennings Bryan Dorn, H. R. Gross, and Thomas Dodd put out to pasture this fall. And it might be great fun to work in the campaigns of such outspoken liberal doves as Shirley Chilholm, Phil Burton, and William Fitts Ryan. Forget it. Remember the ducks. It would probably be more comfortable to hunt ducks from your front porch, but if you are serious about victory you avoid the hopeless cause and the sure thing. Enthusiasm is not enough. To win, we must carefully focus and direct our resources.

Power in the Committees   One other form of selectivity should also be emphasized. The real work of Congress is done in its standing committees. Not all committees are equally important. Nor are all committee members equally powerful. Most of the important, nationally significant bills in both houses of Congress are funnelled through the same four or five standing committees: Appropriations; Armed Services; Ways and Means; Education and Labor (Labor and Public Welfare in the Senate); Judiciary; and Foreign Affairs (Foreign Relations in the Senate). Members of these key committees deserve to be singled out for special attention. Senator Albert Gore of Tennessee, for example, has been both an articulate Southern moderate and, in his positions on both Finance and Foreign Relations committees, one of the nation's most effective fighters for peace and economic justice.

Power within each committee is determined by seniority. The more senior members of the majority party are the most powerful members of each committee. The most senior member in years of service on the committee is automatically the chairman. For the first time since the New Deal, liberals are in a good position, particularly in the Senate, to benefit from the seniority rule. Gore is third-ranking on Finance, Stuart Symington third from the top on Armed Services. Harrison Williams, if reelected from New Jersey, will become chairman of Labor and Public Welfare. As Southern elections become more competitive, the stranglehold that Southerners have held on these key positions will be increasingly loosened.

7

WHAT CAN WE DO IN 1970?

The American political system is amazingly vulnerable to the machinations of dedicated minorities. That these minorities have been more often devoted to the advancement of private rather than public interests is both an indicator and a cause of the current crisis. It is in your power to reverse this imbalance.

<u>Putting Student Power to Work</u> Many of the volumteer activists who worked in the presidential campaign of 1968 and the Congressional primaries of 1970 were students. All recent polls show a clear and unmistakable pattern of anti-student sentiment in the general population. The Movement for a New Congress' postelection poll in New Jersey's Middlesex County reveals, however, that this backlash is directed more against student demostrators than against students per se, and is of negligible importance as regards student canvassers. This is likely to be particularly true if the student presents himself not as part of any student movement but as a representative of a candidate for Congress. Indeed, this is useful advice for all campaign workers. Remember, you are the voter's contact with the campaign. You may be his only link to the candidate. It is your job to represent your candidate's views fully and accurately.

<u>Contacting Voters</u> What can you expect in contacting voters? Perhaps this can best be explained by a quotation from the University of Michigan's Survey Research Center study of the 1958 congressional campaign:

> Of the people who lived in districts where the House seat was contested in 1958, 59%--well over half--said that they had neither read nor heard anything about either candidate for Congress, and less than one in five felt that they knew something about both candidates.

Incumbents, of course, enjoyed a special advantage:

> In districts where an incumbent was opposed for reelection in 1958, 39% of our respondents knew something about the Congressman, whereas only 20% said they knew anything at all about his nonincumbent opponent.

If you are working for a nonincumbent, the chances are that four of every five voters you meet will have heard nothing about your candidate. From their perspective, <u>you</u> <u>are</u> <u>the</u> <u>campaign</u>.

Depressing as these statistics may be from the perspective of democratic theory, they can be very comforting to the candidate who is able to mobilize masses of volunteer campaigners. Resistant as the typical apolitical citizen is to billboards, broadsides, and the media, he can hardly ignore the message of a personal visit. If you can make a credible and creative presentation, and if you can drag these voters to the polls, you probably have won a vote.

Educating Voters   This massive public ignorance most distinguishes Congressional campaigns from presidential ones. Students, we know, played a key role in the 1968 Democratic primaries. But McCarthy's army failed to win the nomination for its candidate, and it failed to win a number of key primaries. In Indiana and California, where it failed most dramatically, it was beaten largely by Robert Kennedy's effective use of TV spots and other mass media communications. In these contests, indeed in most presidential campaigns, most people have heard of both candidates and know something about each. McCarthy's canvassers in 1968, unlike those who will work in Congressional campaigns this fall, were confronted by a public that already had rather definite attitudes toward the major candidates. Volunteer activists are only part of a presidential campaign. As sources of information they must compete with television, radio, and the press. This is true to a lesser degree of Senatorial contests, particularly in the cases of prominent national leaders like Muskie and Mansfield, but it is almost never true of contests for the House.

Party Apathy   Another factor makes House and Senate races more vulnerable to volunteer efforts: the relative lack of concern for Congress generally expressed by regular party organizations. In the words of former Senator Joseph Clark, "concern for the Presidency in national elections and concern with state and local offices, particularly executive offices with their attendant patronage and fund-raising perquisites, come close to exhausting the attention of the regular party organization." Clark learned his lesson the hard way from a party stalwart who bluntly told him to "never mind all that stuff that goes on in Washington. What about jobs in the Highway Department?"

The point is simply that for those who are interested in "all that stuff that goes on in Washington," the field is open. It is open in particular to those who remember the three basic rules of volunteer activism:

1. Don't be easily discouraged.
2. Keep your eye upon the donut and not upon the hole. Make victory your goal.
3. Focus energy by hunting where the ducks are.

ACTIVISM OFFERS SOME DIVIDENDS

Politics is a deadly serious game that is fun. Even the losers get some rewards.

Some of you will be unable to go where the ducks are; there are, for example, no marginal races in Mississippi or North Dakota. In the course of two or three campaigns, however, it is possible to turn a district around. You can build an organization of experienced volunteers, groom candidates who have a chance, and educate and redirect the electorate. With this kind of activity in the district, you may even be surprised to find some of the most militant hawks beginning to change their tune. When President Nixon sent troops into Cambodia, Congressman Ed Patten of New Jersey concluded "after a long and sleepless night" that he would have to support the President's decision. Tow days later, 200 student volunteers went into Middlesex County to work for Patten's primary opponent, Lew Kaden. The next day, Patten reconsidered his stand and accused Nixon of a "tragic blunder" in sending American soldiers to Cambodia.

Even New York's most hawkish Congressman, John Rooney, was moved during his primary race against Peter Eikenberry to introduce a resolution in the House limiting our involvement in Cambodia. "Candidates," as James Reston wrote in the New York Times on June 2, "are not impervious to philosophy, but they are more interested in votes." Too many of those interested in peace, he continued, "have not yet learned the first rule of effective lobbying, which is to put themselves in the candidate's place and make their objectives relevant to the man's main aim of reelection."

YOU CAN HELP DECIDE

Citizen power in a democracy is located in the ballot box. Whether your candidate wins or loses, you can help decide the future of American politics. Campaign activity provides as good an opportunity as our system allows to encourage meaningful dialogue between citizens of differing points of view. It stands as the single most effective form of lobbying yet devised. It is the best possible counter to the distorting effects of big money in political campaigns. It is the breeding ground for long-range change: in these grass-roots volunteer efforts, the results of the 1972 Congressional and presidential campaigns will be determined.

Student volunteers have already had an impact on primary contests in such states as New York, California, and South Dakota. They have been most successful when working on behalf of incumbents with regular party organizations and in districts where there has been no incumbent. Chapter 2 is an analysis of one of the first primaries to involve massive volunteer efforts. The results were in many ways discouraging, but there are lessons to be learned from defeat that can contribute to an understanding of how volunteer efforts can be channelled most effectively.

2
What Can Volunteer Activity Mean?

Early in 1970, Lew Kaden, a young attorney, decided to challenge incumbent Congressman Edward Patten for the Democratic nomination in New Jersey's 15th Congressional District. Before the upsurge in student interest after the Cambodian invasion, Kaden had waged an essentially conventional campaign although he clearly marked himself off as a dove and a challenger of the entrenched party organization in Middlesex County. Kaden appealed to a varied group of liberals: supporters of Henry Helstoski's unsuccessful try for the New Jersey gubernatorial nomination in 1969, remnants of the New Jersey Democratic Coalition, and local people dissatisfied with the "ins" in the county.

THE KADEN CAMPAIGN

In early May, Kaden found himself with hundreds of volunteer workers provided largely through the Movement for a New Congress. Because it was impossible to get lists of registered voters by party affiliation, the Kaden organizers decided to undertake a comprehensive door-to-door canvass in order to find out where voters were located who would support their man. Emphasis was also placed on persuading the uncommitted to vote for Kaden. To some extent, then, an "issue" canvass took place in which canvassers talked to the voters, primarily about the Indochina War.

Middlesex County was not an ideal district for student canvassers, nor for a militant dove. While the Congressional District includes the university areas surrounding Rutgers and a number of new suburban communities with essentially well-educated, middle-class voters, it also includes older townships that are mostly blue-collar and have strong ethnic components. Important pockets of blacks, Puerto Ricans, and Jews live in the district, but Patten and the regular organization have been reasonably responsive to these groups, in terms of both policy and patronage, and have thus retained the support of significant numbers.

Kaden had hoped to get around 14,000 votes in a low turnout year, since there was only a Senate primary and no gubernatorial primary. He hoped that his number would carry him to victory. The final vote was Patten, 24,650, to Kaden, 12,660. Thus, although Kaden came near his hoped-for total, he was beaten badly, getting around 34% of the vote.

Why Did Kaden Lose? The campaign attracted a great deal of local and national publicity. Because it was seen as a test case for the

Movement and for student participation in general, it was covered by
Life, _Look_, the national press, and CBS. Many people offered interpre-
tations after the fact. Some columnists argued that student participation had hurt Kaden, that he had been expected to do much better. Kaden
supporters noted that Kaden was an unknown before the campaign; that he
was up against a popular Congressman who had partially defused the war
issue by moving precipitously toward a dovish stand after Cambodia. Moreover, Kaden's vote was about 50% greater than any liberal insurgent candidate had ever received in the district.

THE LESSONS OF DEFEAT

     Whatever the relative merits of these arguments, the Kaden campaign
did provide an excellent opportunity to assess the impact of massive
volunteer effort on a difficult race. The Movement for a New Congress
was particularly anxious to evaluate the role of students. Answers to
such questions as whether the volunteer efforts had hurt or helped Kaden
were essential to planning future operations. The poll devised to get
at these questions was planned, developed, supervised, and analyzed by
experienced volunteers working on their own time. The results were most
revealing and tell us much about the ways in which volunteers can be
used most effectively.*

     The relatively small size of the sample makes the detailed analysis
that followed a guide more than a final answer. It is a useful guide,
however, because the public opinion survey was carefully drawn up and
carried out and because light does seem to be thrown on important issues
at stake.

     The poll aimed at finding out:

     1. Was there anything to the notion of a backlast against student
participation in the campaign?
     2. What was the issue content, if any, in the voting breakdown?
     3. Had student canvassing increased voter turnout, and if so, in
what direction?

     Voters React to Student Volunteers The Kaden poll provides conclu-
sive evidence to dispell the notion of backlash against student participation in the campaign. Whatever their attitudes toward student protest
in general, when asked what they thought of the idea of students becoming
involved in electoral politics, 71% of those polled said it was a good
idea, compared with 13% who said it was a bad idea and 16% who weren't
sure. Among the Patten voters, 71% said it was a good idea, only 10%
were opposed, and 19% weren't sure. Only 2% of the respondents said
they would vote against the candidate the college students were campaigning for.

*Compilation of data and analysis of results were handled by Mike
Rappaport, Jay Katz, and Sue Gunzelman of the Opinion Research Corporation, Princeton. The questionaire used for the telephone poll
was constructed by Herb Abelson and Len Newton of the Princeton-
based Response Analysis Corporation. The individuals acted in a
volunteer capacity, and their place of work is mentioned for iden-
tification purposes only.

<u>Why</u> <u>Voters</u> <u>Chose</u> <u>As</u> <u>They</u> <u>Did</u> In the poll, voters gave substantially different reasons for voting for Kaden than for voting for Patten. 45% of the Kaden voters said they voted for him because it was time for a change, because new blood and young ideas were needed; 43% of the Kaden voters specifically mentioned the war issue as their reason for voting for Kaden, and 12% said they voted for him because they agreed with his policies. None of the reasons given for voting for Kaden were given as reasons for voting for Patten.

Half of Patten voters said they voted for him because he had experience or had done a good job; 23% said they liked him, had received personal assistence from him, or were voting against the other candidate; and 20% said they voted for Patten because they knew him. These reasons point up the advantage typically held by the incumbent Congressman.

REASONS FOR VOTING FOR CANDIDATE

	Patten	Kaden
Experience; good job	50%	0%
Like him; personal assistance; voted against other candidate	23	8
Know him	20	7
Time for a change; new blood; young ideas	0	45
War issue	0	43
Agree with policy	--*	12
Other	12	7
No answer	2	0

*Less and ½%

Percentages add to more than 100% of multiple answers.

<u>Views</u> <u>on</u> <u>Vietnam</u> A substantial difference existed between Patten and Kaden voters' views on American policy in Vietnam. Of those voters who favored the withdrawal of American troops from Vietnam as soon as possible, 56% voted for Kaden and 44% voted for Patten. Of those voters supporting President Nixon's policy of staying in Vietnam until South Vietnam can defend itself, the overwhelming majority (77%) voted for Patten, and only 23% voted for Kaden.

13

THE VOTE AND VIETNAM POLICY

Voted for	Withdraw	Stay and fight
Patten	44%	77%
Kaden	56	23

THE EFFECTS OF CANVASSING

The major conclusion to be drawn from the Kaden poll is that the effect of canvassing depends heavily on the inherent political attitudes of the area canvassed. Student canvassers can have only very limited success in persuading voters to vote for their particular candidate, or in getting them to adopt their view on any given issue. The main effect that canvassers can have is to identify favorable voters and help pull them out on Election Day.

Where Not to Use Student Canvassers The poll data suggest that it is not wise for student canvassers to concentrate on areas known to be generally favorable to the candidate and/or his views. In such areas, the candidate may well be able to find indigenous workers attund to the voting attitudes of individuals in their districts. Additional canvassing of such areas by nonindigenous students does not only **appear** to be not useful; it seems to be definitely detrimental. The effect seems to be to pull out opposition voters who would otherwise not be contacted by anyone, since the opposing forces will not usually have adequate indigenous manpower in these districts.

In short, canvassing such areas is superfluous in pulling out favorable voters, and also serves to pull out opposition voters. This does not mean that individual students shouldn't be put to work (under local direction) in such areas, especially on Election Day. But the data clearly indicate that outside volunteers must coordinate their activities very closely with local groups.

Working in decidedly unfavorable areas seems to be marginally useful at best. The effect of canvassing these areas may well be to increase the total opposing plurality (though not the opposing percentage), since most of the people contacted will be unfavorable and some would not otherwise vote.

Where Student Canvassers Can Help Student canvassers will be most effective, the data from the Kaden poll seem to indicate, if they concentrate their efforts in marginally favorable to marginally unfavorable areas where the opposition is known to be at least somewhat organized and where the candidate being supported has little local organization. The opposition reaches and pulls out its certain voters in such areas, in any case, when the candidate the students support is not the incumbent. Contacting voters thus does not run such a high risk of pulling opposition voters to the polls. Such areas should be covered fully. Do not go through the area just once, missing all those not at home. Assign the same canvassers, if possible, to cover the same area several times.

... And How Canvassers should spend much of their time and effort attempting to find local workers in marginal areas. Getting the help of one good local neighbor is worth more than knocking on 25 doors. Because time was limited, the Kaden campaign did not pay nearly enough attention to briefing canvassers on this approach. Canvassers should call on all those people who have shown a willingness to work, and they should volunteer to help the local person set up an organization in which college students providing much of the manpower under the local person's direction. In short, they should stress the use of canvassers as aids in the building of a local organization, not simply as flying squads moving through (and out of) an area.

About 13% of the voters in the Democratic primary thought that contact by college students had some effect on their vote--11% said a favorable effect, and 2% said an unfavorable effect. If these data are taken at face value, they indicate a net gain of about 9% in Kaden's vote as a result of the college students' efforts. However, just about half of those who claimed that the students had had a favorable effect voted for Patten anyway.

This evidence from the Kaden poll, though limited, when considered along with other analyses, indicates that student canvassers in a Democratic Congressional primary can persuade enough voters to produce a 2% to 6% gain for their candidate. In a well-conducted campaign, college students doing carefully selected canvassing might produce gains of as much as 8% to 10% in a particular campaign. Given the marginal nature of the races in which the Movement has decided to work, these percentages are very significant.

Some of the obstacles that Kaden had to surmount, of course, were peculiar to his campaign. Not having access to party registration lists made it unusually difficult for him to locate target areas. Student volunteers entered the campaign too late to participate in an attempt to register new voters. Above all, it was a primary race rather than a general election. This gave Kaden no hard core of party voters whose loyalty he could take for granted. He had to build his constituency from scratch against an opponent whose eight years of service had earned him numerous personal friends in the district.

3
Adding New Voters to the Rolls

Textbooks teach us to think of voting as an important privilege of a democracy. Nonvoting is deplored as an abdication of civic responsibility. In the 1968 presidential elections, however, four of every ten Americans of voting age did not avail themselves of that right. In the 1970 Congressional elections it is highly unlikely that half of the eligible electorate will actually vote. Some of these nonvoters, perhaps as many as 20%, are legally disenfranchised as aliens, felons, or morons, or because they fail to meet state and local residency requirements. The vast majority, however, choose to be nonvoters. Who are these silent minorities, and why have they chosen to remain outside of the electoral process?

Who Doesn't Vote? A number of social scientists have identified the demographic characteristics of the people who are least likely to vote. Most agree in listing the young, blacks, the poor, the less well educated, women, and people in rural areas. From a practical perspective, a list like this one helps to identify target groups: in conducting a registration drive, young people, blacks, and so on, constitute obvious target communities. Answers to the question why people refuse to vote, however, are probably more important to the conduct of a successful registration drive.

Few volunteer activities could be more important in marginal districts than registration. This chapter describes a strategy for adding new voters to the rolls. Before going into the specific details of how to do it, we have tried to present a theory of nonvoting, to explain why so many Americans do not exercise their right to vote. What we are tryint to do in these introductory pages is to prepare the volunteer activist for contact with the apathetic by explaining some possible motivating factors.

A COST-GAINS CALCULUS OF VOTING

Anthony Downs has suggested that "every rational man decides to vote just as he makes all other decisions: if the returns outweigh the costs, he votes; if not, he abstains."[1] Whether or not you consider the typical nonvoter a rational man, this assumption provides a useful starting point for an analysis of nonvoting.

Let us look first at the "costs" of voting. In every state but North Dakota and Alaska the act of voting must be preceded by the act of regis-

16

tering. In some parts of the country this task is confusing, difficult, and time-consuming. When, for example, the registration office is open only on weekdays from 9 to 4, registering means taking time off from work for the average citizen. When inadequate facilities are provided, registering may mean substantial personal inconvenience. As one New York City resident said in 1964, "I sure do want to vote against that man (Barry Goldwater), but I don't think I hate him enough to stand on that line all day long."[2]

Time is the most obvious cost of voting. In low income areas, however, many residents see the costs in more tangible terms. One of the most difficult jobs of registering voters in some neighborhoods is convincing people that registration does not subject them to new taxes, new debt obligations, or other financial responsibilities. Remember that people in these areas are likely to be highly suspicious of contacts with government.

Down's cost-gains theory of nonvoting gets considerable support in a study by Stanley Kelley, Jr., Richard E. Ayres, and William G. Rowen in the June 1967 issue of the <u>American</u> <u>Political</u> <u>Science</u> <u>Review</u>. Kelley and his colleagues found that "local differences in the turnout for elections are to a large extent related to local differences in the rules governing, and arrangements for handling, the registration of voters." The more difficult it is to register, in other words, the higher the proportion of nonvoters.

Laws that make it difficult to register and vote are particularly intimidating to those with the least education. Where the costs of voting are highest, differences in turnout between low and high education groups are greatest. This suggests that the poorly educated may frequently be nonvoters partly because they are unaware of or intimidated by the procedures necessary to register.

<u>Cost-Gains</u> <u>and</u> <u>Registration</u> Insofar as some kind of cost-gains calculus can be used to explain nonvoting, the goals of a registration drive should clearly be:

1. To lower the costs of voting by making it as easy as possible to register and vote.
2. To increase the perceived benefits by convincing potential voters of the importance of the impending electoral contests.

We shall return to specific suggestions along these lines later in this chapter.

NONVOTING AND SOCIAL PRESSURE

Not all decisions to vote or not to vote are based on rational calculations. Even in Australia, where registration is automatic and nonvoters must pay a fine, 3% or 4% of those eligible do not vote. Morris Rosenberg in a fascinating series of interviews found that political apathy was related to various forms of social pressure. Some nonvoters, for example, viewed involvement in the political process as a potential threat to more important social relationships. Lack of political involvement was explained in ways like these:

Right now I want to avoid friction--we were just married last June--

so we try not to get into political disucssions.

I think it's better to do something that has direct results....
(In politics) you don't get any direct results. In Girl Scouts, you
see the results; you have a chance to shape the character of the
girls. I think that's more important.

People like to be entertained... and get away from the troubles of
the day; and if you get them to start worrying about England and
France and everything else in the world, they're just not interested.[3]

In trying to register voters, you will probably encounter some who will
actively resist even the suggestion of involvement. Some radicals, some
alienated individuals, quite a few who find politics too dull and unin-
teresting to merit their attention may never be brought to the polls.

The United States is not a very political nation. Few Americans
are active in politics, and for most voting is a relatively trivial
decision. It is your job to make the decision to vote less trivial.
Nothing, of course, can substitute for a good candidate and an exciting
campaign to motivate the normally apathetic; but in many instances candidates and campaigns are too remote from everyday experience to serve
as catalysts to action. The key to voter registration is often social
pressure. People vote because they are embarrassed not to, because
their neighbors do, because it is accepted as one of the duties of a
loyal American, or simply because someone asks them to. One reason that
upper- and middle-income citizens are more likely to vote than the poor
is that social pressures encouraging voting are much stronger in more
affluent communities. Successful voter-registration drives often depend,
therefore, on successful interpersonal contacts. This is one reason for
preferring the door-to-door campaign to telephone contacts.

SELECTIVE REGISTRATION AND ELECTORAL SUCCESS

Something in the democratic spirit is satisfied by bringing a new
voter to the polls. Generally speaking, however, altruism and democratic
ideals have little to do with effective registration drives. "The candidate who is deadly serious about winning," Larry O'Brien wrote in the
Democratic campaign manual for 1964, "is always concerned about registration."[4] Or, as Ern Reynolds told the participants at a Republican
campaign management seminar in 1966, voter registration is "a strategic
maneuver.... The nonregistrants represent the unsolf market, the people
who have not been reached by politics yet, and who very badly need to be
reached. These unregistered people represent power waiting to be seized."
Even if a thorough registration drive was conducted two years ago, it
needs to be done again. Since 1968, nine million Americans have turned
21. Thirty-two million have moved and must re-register. In every Congressional district in the country there are, right now, something between 30,000 and 100,000 eligible voters who are not properly registered.

Strategies for Registration There are two principle strategies of
registration. The first is highly selective, focusing on areas of antici-
pated party or candidate strength. The second assumes that new voters
are likely to be particularly susceptible to the appeals of those who first
contact them about voting. Its goal is simply to register as many new
voters as possible. The second strategy has been most frequently used

by Democratic candidates, for some surveys have shown between 70% and 80% of the unregistered will lean toward the Democratic party. The utility of such surveys is open to question, however, for they also show unregistered citizens to be ill-informed about politics, apathetic, and highly susceptible to emotional appeals. It is quite possible, given these findings, that unregistered people lean toward the Democratic party but vote that way only when contacted and registered by Democratic workers. Saturation strategies may work for either party.

Whichever strategy is used, the first step is to identify target communities. This can be done on a demographic basis or, preferably, in terms of actual voting patterns in the district. If you are using the selective approach in a Republican campaign, you start with the most heavily Republican election districts and work down the list. Democrats, of course, begin in Democratic areas. The logic of this technique is simply that most people--particularly those of low partisan loyalties-- are likely to vote as their neighbors do. Most nonvoters do not have strong attachments to either party. Lacking such commitments and lacking both interest in and knowledge of public affairs, they are highly sus- ceptible to social pressure. If they live in Democratic neighborhoods, these pressures are likely to be Democratic, and in Republican areas Republican. In an effective registration drive, therefore, we follow the rule outlined in Chapter 1 of hunting ducks where the ducks are.

If saturation strategies are used, going where the ducks are means zeroing in on districts where new voters are likely to be most heavily concentrated. First priority is given to those precincts where com- parisons of population and registration figures show that the proportion of unregistered citizens is highest. The obvious practical advantage of this approach over the selective approach is that it greatly increases the likelihood of making contact with large numbers of new voters.

THE NUTS AND BOLTS OF REGISTRATION

Identifying the Target An selective registration drive that is to be effective begins with paper work. The better the research, the easier the follow-through. Research consists of identifying target areas and locating the unregistered. Identify target areas by using party regis- tration lists or, if such lists are unavailable from the registrar of voters, by examining past voting behavior. Once the data are assembled, rank the districts simply in order either of aggregate party votes or of percentage advantages. First priority then goes, in a Democratic drive, to those districts with the highest numbers or proportions of Democrats.

Door-to-Door-Canvassing Once target areas have been identified, estimate the potential for registration, and locate specifically the un- registered voters. If manpower permits, a house-to-house canvass is the most thorough and reliable means of achieving this objective. If man- power is limited--and it usually is--registry lists can be compared with city directories, jury lists, electric company lists, or reverse-order phone books that list a neighborhood's households by street address. Registration goals can then be set and canvassers sent to specific house- holds which are known to contain people who are not registered to vote.

As a useful organizational device at this point, set a quota for each volunteer. Experience shows that 20 is a reasonable number. To the ambitious, this may sound low. With call-backs, reminders, and transportation figured in, however, one volunteer will find it very difficult to be responsible for the behavior of more than 20 to 25 nonvoters. Those who work quickly can always be given a second list to cover in another district. Teams of two--preferably male and female--are most effective in door-to-door campaigns. In non-English-speaking districts, one of each canvassing pair should speak the native language.

Liaison It is always wise in a political campaign to establish liaison with other groups that may share your goals. The League of Women Voters, though nonpartisan in approach, can be very helpful in providing research help on local laws and volunteers to work in certain districts. Labor unions are often active in registration work.

Most important is contact with the regular party organization. District committeemen and women--or percinct captains as they are called in many states--are supposed to be familiar with every resident of their districts. If most of them actually were, there would of course be no need for registration drives. Even the laziest of district leaders, however, can be of some assistance to nonresident volunteers. Your first stop should be at the home of the district leader to check your list of names against his or her knowledge of his neighbors. Don't be surprised, however, if district leaders prove uncooperative. By suggesting that the district may contain unregistered members of his party, you are implicitly criticizing his performance as a party leader. Tact and diplomacy may prove useful, but you should never lose sight of your goal of enrolling new voters.

Briefing Volunteer canvassers must be thoroughly briefed before they go out to register voters. In most states the League of Women Voters publishes a guide to election laws. Each canvasser should know these laws upside down and backward. Nothing is more annoying to the potential voter than traveling to the clerk's office only to find that he cannot register without first producing proof of age, or naturalization, or whatever else the state law may require. Handbills or cards that list important laws, give times and places of registration, and provide a phone contact for further information should be carried by each canvasser. Volunteer headquarters should also provide back-up support for canvassers in the form of transportation and baby-sitting pools and access to legal counsel if called for.

Telephone Canvassing The most efficient (though not the most thorough) method of performing a registration canvass is by phone. A reverse-order phone book, organized by street address, can conveniently be compared with voter registration lists to make initial contacts. In some neighborhoods, such as those with apartments guarded by doormen, personal access may be limited and telephone contact the only means of entry.

Door-to-door canvassing, however, is by far the preferable alternative and generally worth the added manpower costs. This is true, first, because of the growing trend toward the use of unlisted phones. In New York City, for example, one subscriber in four has an unlisted number. Twenty percent of the total nationwide population, moreover, has no phone. Second, direct personal contact is more effective. Studies show that it is "much easier to refuse over the phone than it is to refuse a request in face-to-face situations"; and that the not-at-homes are apparently not reduced appreciably by the phone call, which would be its main justification."

<u>What</u> <u>the</u> <u>Canvasser</u> <u>Wants</u> <u>to</u> <u>Achieve</u> In contacting voters, whether by phone or in person, the goals of the canvasser are to lessen the perceived costs of voting and to increase the perceived benefits. Lessening the costs means making it as convenient as the law allows to register and vote. Offers to provide baby-sitters and transportation will lower the costs for some voters. For many, getting information is one of the costs that can be reduced or eliminated; you can save these citizens the time and effort of finding out whether or not they are eligible, where and when they can register, and so on. Increasing the perceived benefits means relating the upcoming election to candidates or issues that are important to the individual in question. Social pressure may also be used as a motivating appeal--"Tomorrow," you might say, "I'm taking your neighbors the Smiths to the registrar. May I take you too?"

APPROACHING THE NONVOTER

Before any doorbells are rung, the campaign organization should have identified target precincts and set quotas. It should have established liaison with other groups working on registration to avoid duplication of effort. It should have thoroughly briefed each volunteer. It should have acquired legal counsel and made contact with volunteers for baby-sitting and transporting potential voters to the registrar. It should have provided each volunteer with campaign brochures, cards, or throwaways outlining local laws, "hard cards" for recording information (these are described in greater detail in Chapter 4), a map of the district to be covered, a list of registered and unregistered citizens in the district, application forms for absentee ballots, change-of-address cards, and a clipboard for holding everything together.

Thus armed, the volunteer approaches his target. It goes without saying that you should be neat in appearance and harmonious with your surroundings--don't wear a tuxedo in approaching a hard-hat. You should, of course, be courteous, patient but efficient, well-informed, and not patronizing. You should know what you're talking about.

<u>What</u> <u>Does</u> <u>the</u> <u>Canvasser</u> <u>Say</u>? Market research clearly indicates that the natural approach is best. People are quick to spot a put-on or set speech, and they are easily turned off by such an approach. Each volunteer will, with practice, develop his or her own particular line of attack. Role-playing sessions, in which volunteers alternate playing the parts of newly transplanted voters, radicals who don't believe in working within the system, or new voters who know nothing about registration laws or the impending elections, are useful warm-ups, but no substitute for on-the-job experience.

You may use as a basic guide the following interview outline adopted from a Democratic party campaign manual:

Before you set out: Using the map and registry list, plan your itinerary. Fill out the names, addresses, and phone numbers on the hard cards for each household you plan to visit.

When you call on a family or visit them, be as brief as possible. Limit your talk to something like the following:

Hello, is this Mrs. Warren Harding?

Mrs. Harding, I'm Nick Sutton from the_____for Congress Committee. I'm doing some volunteer work for the_____ (name of candidate) campaign. We're trying to get in touch with all the Democrats in this neighborhood. Do you have a moment? (If she says no, thank her and ask when you may call back later.) If she says "Well, I'm a Republican," go ahead and ask her the questions for Republicans (numbers 4 and 5).

3. If she says yes, say, "Would you mind telling me if you are a Republican or a Democrat?"

A. If she says Republican mark an R on the hard card and go on to questions 4 and 5.

B. If she says Independent ask, "Do you think yourself closer to the Democratic or Republican Party most of the time?" If she says Democratic, mark the card ID. If she says neither, leave the "I" to stand alone. If she says Republican mark the card IR and go to questions 4 and 5.

4. This question is for Republicans and Independent Republicans only: Are there any other people 21 or over in your house?

5. (This question too is only for those leaning toward the opposite party): Are any of them Democrats? (If there are, ask their names, write them down, and find out how you can get in touch with them.) Terminate the interview with a courteous good-by.

6. If the answer to question 3 is Democrat or leaning Democratic, "May I have your full name? Phone numbers?" (Write these down or correct any errors on your card.)

7. If you are working from a registry list, and Mrs. Harding's name is not on it, ask if you can provide assistance. Frequently a voter who is not on the registry list will insist that she is in fact registered. Sometimes this is because the registry lists are not up to date; ask when the voter registered. More often, it is because the voter has moved or been purged from the rolls. Asking "When did you last vote from this address?" will usually elicit the necessary information. If she hasn't voted in two years (four in some states, one in others)or has moved since voting, consult your Registration Information Card and tell her if she has to register again or file change of address notice.

8. "Are there any other eligible voters in your house? Anyone about to turn 21? Any who will turn 18 in 1971 after the new voting law goes into effect? If "Yes," list each one on your form. Then ask questions 6 and 7 about each one and enter the replies. Note that roomers or relatives may have separate phones.

9. "Does any member of your household who is eligible to vote happen to be in the armed services, or away from home in school or on a job or in a hospital? Will anyone be away on election day?"

10. If "Yes," "May I give you (or send him) a request form for an absentee ballot?" This can be very important. An average of 20 to 30 persons in each election district in the country who are eligible to vote absentee do not. One reason is that the deadline for applying is so far in advance of the election that most people simply forget.

Just as the absentees swung California to Richard Nixon in 1960, they may well provide a margin of victory in many races this fall. There are few better opportunities for picking up sure votes for your candidate than the careful distribution of absentees forms.

11. If the person seems quite interested, ask, "Would you be willing to put in a few hours a week on volunteer work for the party, as I am doing? Can you do phoning from your home? Would you be willing to host a coffee for our candidate?" Record this information carefully, and be sure to call back those who express an interest. No volunteer can be as effective as the one who actually lives in the neighborhood.

12. "Thank you very much Mrs. Harding. We will add your name, if you don't mind, to our mailing lists, and would appreciate your talking to your neighbors about the_____campaign. Good-by."

If you are working for a Republican candidate, of course, you must vary this procedure accordingly. If you are working for an individual candidate rather than the entire party ticket, you may want to ask questions which refer specifically to support for that candidate. In a registration canvass, however, the strictly partisan approach is probably best. In off-year elections most voters vote the straight ticket. More important, they are more likely to have some notion of what the party label means than they are to have heard anything about an individual candidate.

<u>Special Registration Laws</u>   In some states, any registered voter may become a deputy registrar empowered actually to enroll voters in their homes. In others, mobile registration units visit various communities with special evening hours for registration. Needless to say, you should make every effort to coordinate with these activities. Appendix C gives basic information about registration and voting laws for most states.

<u>Special Target Groups</u>   Registration drives keyed to special target groups may work well in some districts. Labor union lists and lists of students and faculty members at local universities can be used to good advantage. Students are a particularly sticky problem. In many areas they are effectively disenfranchised by local clerks who insist that college dorms do not constitute legal residences for purposes of voting. Graduate students who have left home may find this a difficult problem. Registering students at the county seat, through deputy registrars, or at mobile registration--where they may not be known as students--may provide one means of evading recalcitrant local clerks. If this tactic does not work, be sure to see that students make every effort to register at home and to vote by absentee ballot. In about half the states, registration by mail is permitted (see Appendix C). Students may vote by absentee ballot in all states but Mississippi, provided that they apply well in advance. The potential number of such votes is very large. Your work in bringing them out may be vital to other New Congress candidates throughout the country.

FOLLOWING THROUGH AFTER REGISTRATION

The registration drive is the opening gun of the door-to-door campaign. It is not an isolated exercise in good citizenship, but an integral part of any effective election strategy. It has two goals: registering new voters, and compiling information for later activities. In this second aspect it overlaps with the canvassing efforts described in Chapter 4. Most of the guidelines set out there for effective canvassing techniques also apply to registration. Any bits of information acquired in registering new voters should be carefully recorded for future use.

The registration drive serves as a shakedown cruise for the volunteer staff. It is a good place to spot weaknesses in the organization, and it serves to initiate the volunteer to the art of canvassing. If it is to be effective, it must be carefully planned. To reduce the costs of voting, volunteers must know the election laws.

They must be backed up by transportation and baby-sitting pools. To increase the perceived benefits of voting, volunteers must know the area, the issues, and the candidates. And there must be follow-through: the information compiled by each volunteer must be carefully processed and recorded. Those who need absentee ballots should get them. Those who need transportation should get it. Those who agree to help should be contacted immediately. Once the registration deadline is past, you can't go back again. No matter how much someone wants to vote for your candidate, he cannot do so if he is not registered, and his vote multiplied through every percinct in the district may mark the margin between victory and defeat.

4
Winning Votes

For many years reformers have attacked machine politics with its attendant graft, corruption, and patronage abuses. In many parts of the
country once-powerful machines have been overthrown by dedicated amateurs.
In other areas, they have crumbled and decayed from within; out of touch
with social change, insensitive to the demands of the new politics, and
unable to build new bases of support, the boss-ruled machine is becoming
a political anachronism. In their zeal for displacing boss rule, however, some reform groups have thrown the baby out with the bath water.
They have destroyed the machines, and along with them some of the most
legitimately effective techniques of political activity yet devised.

THE DOOR-TO-DOOR CANVASS

One of these techniques--the systematically organized and coordinated
door-to-door canvass--has seldom been employed by reform candidates.
The door-to-door canvass, the purpose of which is to find, register, and
deliver sympathetic voters to the polls, has been an effective staple of
practical political action for at least the last 150 years. In 1840
Abraham Lincoln urged his party, the Whigs:

> Organize the whole state, so that every Whig can be brought to the
> polls....divide the county into small districts and appoint in each
> a sub-committee..., make a perfect list of voters and ascertain with
> certainty for whom they will vote.... and on election day see that
> every Whig is brought to the polls.[1]

This technique of finding, registering, and bringing your supporters
to the polls has been used successfully over the years by Plunkitt of
Tammany, Boss Tweed, and Mayor Daley. Yet strangely, progressives have
seldom employed careful, precinct-by-precinct organization. Even the
McCarthy campaign, while very effective in door-to-door activities, was
only infrequently organized at the precinct level in such a way as to
make most effective use of the canvass.

The reasons for this failure are probably connected with the more dis-
tasteful aspects of machine operations. However, there is no reason volunteers working for an ideal cannot be as effectively organized as ward-
heelers receiving a political boss's patronage. Very few elections have
been bought or stolen. They have been won by those forces possessing
the largest sympathetic audience and the superior organization necessary

to mobilize that audience and bring a large proportion of it to the polls. Organization, not fraud, is the keyword. Often, if liberals were organized as well as or better than their opposition (that is, tightly organized down to the precinct level), they would have won. However, quite often, knowing that they were not, liberals used the few but all too apparent vacant lot and cemetery voters as convenient whipping boys for their own lack or organization. No doubt votes are sometimes stolen. Elections, however, are not usually stolen. They are won by efficient organizations.

HOW TO ORGANIZE AN EFFECTIVE CANVASS

<u>Organizing the Precinct</u> Efficient organization begins with the delineation of simple functional tasks, first within a particular geographic area. In order to facilitate the finding, registering, and bringing of sympathetic voters to the polls, subdivide, the Congressional District into smaller, more manageable units, usually precincts. This limits the territory to be covered and enhances local contact with the voter.

Appoint chairmen for each of the small units (precincts, boxes, or election districts), which usually contain 100 to 1,000 voters. Appointing a precinct leader or chairman establishes the local link in the chain of command and ties the district-wide headquarters to the grass-roots efforts of precinct volunteers.

Hold an organizational and training meeting to ensure that each precinct chairman understands his duties clearly and knows how to set up a precinct organization. Provide the chairmen with detailed maps of your locality, often available from Chamber of Commerce, businesses, and utility companies. The local Western Union office is often the best place to find out where such maps are available.

<u>Preparing the Hard Card File</u> The precinct chairman's first job is to prepare a list of all voting-age residents of his precinct. This list can be compiled from several sources. First, rely on the list of registered voters (and their party affiliations, if given). Supplement this list by cross-checking against a city directory, tax roll, utility list, or a reverse-order phone book in order to get names of eligible voters who are not registered.

If a registration canvass has been carried out, you already have information on the party preferences of voters registered at that time, and of some other registered voters. This information forms the basis for the "hard card" file that is essential to effective precinct organization. Such a file contains a card for everyone eligible to vote in the precinct-- registered or unregistered. You may devise a color scheme to denote voter preference (Democrat, Republican, undecided) and registration status.

Hard card files should be kept in triplicate--one set by the Congressional campaign headquarters and two by the precinct leader. He arranges ones of the files alphabetically by voter's last name and the other by voter's street address. A sample of such a card is printed below.

Before setting up your own system, you will find it useful to discover whether existing information sources are willing to work with you. Some district leaders from the regular organization may already have up-

to-date files, and a great deal of time can be saved if these regular
organization people are willing to work with volunteers.

ADDRESS:_____

TOWN
or
WARD_____PRECINCT_____

NAME:_____
PARTY PREFERENCE: D   R   I

OCCUPATION:_____
PHONE:_____

NEEDS:
_____ ABSENTEE BALLOT
_____ BABY SITTER
_____ TRANSPORTATION
_____ OTHER

CAN CONTRIBUTE:
_____ FINANCIALLY
_____ HQ WORK
_____ PRECINCT WORK
_____ POLL WATCHING
_____ ELECTION DAY PHONING
_____ OTHER

ADDITIONAL INFO: (e.g., Union member, civil servant, etc.; "likely to
split ticket," will vote late in day; other useful
information)

NEEDS TO BE RECONTACTED: YES   NO

Sending Out Workers Before any volunteers are sent into the field,
make careful preparations. Don't send any canvasser out until he has
been thoroughly briefed on the nature of the area he is covering, the
key issues of the campaign, and information about the candidate. Schedule
briefing sessions on a regular basis. If this is impossible, have volunteers report to single headquarters before being sent into the field.

More important, don't send out any canvasser before the campaign has
made a thorough analysis of the district, aimed at locating target precincts. The usual rule of thumb in selecting such areas is: Go where
you are strongest. The results of the Movement's post-election poll in
New Jersey (see Chapter 2) suggest that this rule might be slightly modi-
fied. If local people have already organized a district, the appearance
of outside volunteers helps to mobilize the opposition. Go, then, where
you are strongest in potential vote but weak in organization. In a general election you can pinpoint such areas by studying registry lists, if
your state registers by party, or past patterns of electoral behavior.
Do not send canvassers into opposition strongholds. Your chances of
scoring converts are slim and will be more than offset by the number of
opposition voters you draw to the polls. Marginal districts, and districts
which historically have displayed wide swings in voting behavior, should
receive particular attention.

Tactics of Canvassing When canvassers actually go into the field,
they should go in pairs, if possible. Even where a local precinct worker
is already available, at least one other person (preferably of the opposite sex) should be sent in to help. Having a helper eases his work
burden somewhat; more important, most people are more receptive to two
women, or to a man and a woman, than they are to one or two strange men.
Moreover, it is easier for two people to make a graceful exit from a
difficult conversation than it is for a lone worker.

If the volunteer cannot get past the door, his time is wasted. Any gimmicks that lessen the suspicious nature of housewives in particular should be employed. This is why a clean-cut appearance, identifying buttons or even hats, decorated clipboards, etc., should be used.

Timing is also important. The best times to find people at home are evenings between 6:30 and 9:30, and Saturdays from 11 A. M. until 5 P. M. More people are at home weeknights than on Saturdays, but they are more likely to give a courteous hearing to canvassers on the weekend than they are at night. Where no one is home, the canvasser should note the time of the attempted contact so he can make his call-back at a different hour. If a registration canvass has already been conducted, assign volunteers for canvassing in the district where they worked for registration.

CONTACTING VOTERS

The objectives of a good canvass are twofold: to gain information and to mobilize lukewarm supporters. You should make absolutely clear to canvassers that their principal job is not to argue issues with the voters, but to evaluate voters in terms of candidate preferences. The emphasis must be on mobilization, not conversion. Arguing issues with voters is bad politics for many reasons. The costs, in terms of wasted time which could be more profitably spent canvassing (evaluating) other voters, are very high.

Several studies have convincingly shown that very few voters are converted by visits from election workers. A recent study by Gerald Kramer of Yale, employing survey data on presidential and Congressional elections from 1952 to 1966, shows that canvassing has little effect on voter preference for national or local offices.[2] Anger created by arguments can cause lackadaisical supporters of your opponent to become mobilized. Such arguments can often lead to misinterpretation of the voter's position (e.g., he may agree with your candidate on the issues you raise but intend to vote for his opponent for other reasons that are more important to him and unknown to you).

Evaluating the Voter "Score" or rate voters on a rating system devised by campaign headquarters. A simple 1-to-5 scale is often best. It rates those voters most favorable to your candidate as 1's, probably favorable as 2's, undecided as 3's, probably against as 4's, and definitely against as 5's. Those whom you have rated as 2's and 3's should be contacted with followup visits to more clearly ascertain their candidate preference. Record these ratings and any appropriate comments, such as the voter's opinions on issues or his special interests, on canvassing sheets that list each resident of the precinct. Wait until you have left the voter's house before writing anything on the canvassing sheet. Later, transfer this information to the voter's hard card in the files.

Approaching the Voter As a canvasser, avoid getting involved in longwinded discussions, even if friendly, unless the person is indicating a willingness to work. If so, pin him down. Will she host a coffee klatch? Make phone calls? Canvass? Get the person's phone number and give it to the campaign manager.

As a canvasser, make yourself informed and read the candidate's literature carefully before you start out. Be prepared to answer questions about his stands on major issues, his background, his chances for election, and so on. If you cannot answer a question, don't guess. Get the person's phone number and promise to get back to him. Make a note of the query, get the answer from campaign headquarters, and call the person back. Even a well-informed canvasser might do well to refer some questions to headquarters, as these call-backs are easily made and indicate interest and concern.

Make your canvass questions subtle and unobtrusive. Indirect questions often elicit information best. But most important, do not argue, evaluate!

Representing Your Candidate   As an effective canvasser, you will do more than simply gather information. For many voters, you will be their only contact with the campaign. It is your job to sell the candidate. But selling in this context does not mean extended argument or debate: the soft sell is most effective. Indeed, simply getting the voter to recognize the candidate's name is half the battle.

The University of Michigan's Survey Research Center study of midterm elections points up very dramatically the impact of name-recognition on voting behavior. The chances are excellent that any given voter will not have heard of either candidate (this was true of 59% of those sampled). If he has heard of only one, the chances are two-to-one that it will be the incumbent. Suppose that you are working for a Democrat against the incumbent Republican. The data in the table suggest the following possible effects of simply impressing voters with the name of the Democratic challenger: for those voters who have heard of neither candidate, name recognition can increase the potential vote of Democratic voters from 92% to 98%, and of those who consider themselves Republicans from 8% to 40%. Among Democrats who are familiar only with the Republican incumbent, name recognition can increase the Democrat's share from 60% to 83%. Even among Republicans who know the name of the incumbent, familarity with the Democratic challenger can increase his share of the vote from 2% to 17%.

What these figures suggest is simply that the issue content of the canvasser's appeal is far less important than conveying the most elementary facts: first, that an election is about to take place, and second, that the name of one of the candidates is the one you are working for. Never mention your opponent by name. Mention your own candidate's name as often as taste permits.

Push the "Brand Name"   One of the first rules of political campaigning is not to get discouraged. One major source of discouragement for many volunteers is the incredibly high level of public apathy and political ignorance. It is important to bear constantly in mind the generally low level of importance which the average citizen attributes to politics and to Congress in particular. Political decisions are low-priority decisions for most people--far less important, say, than the decision to buy a new car.

One attribute of low-priority decisions is that they are highly vulnerable to outside influence. Without meaning to make any invidious comparisons, the voting decisions of many citizens are in some ways comparable to their tooth paste-buying decisions. When he needs tooth-paste, the consumer goes to the store. His objective is to buy tooth-paste: what kind he buys is not important; the decision is a low-priority one. The job of the Colgate company or its ad agency is to inter-cept the consumer somewhere between his home and the store with the name "Colgate." Since the brand-name decision is trivial, and since "Colgate" is the only name that rings a bell, chances are that he will buy Colgate. The voter who gives politics a low priority is similarly inclined to choose the brand-name of the candidate that rings some kind of bell. Canvassers can make those bells ring.

Voting for Own Party Candidate and Other Party Candidate, by Awareness of Candidate

		Voter was aware of		
Voted for Candidate	Both Candidates	Own Party Candidate Only	Other Party Candidate Only	Neither Candidate
Of own party	83%	98%	60%	92%
Of other party	17	2	40	8
Total	100% (N=196)	100% (N=166)	100% (N=68)	100% (N=368)

Source: Donald E. Stokes and Warren E. Miller, "Party Government and the Saliency of Congress," in Angus Campbell, et. al., Elections and the Political Order (New York: John Wiley, 1957), p. 205.

ELECTION DAY

The key to well-run election day activities is good organization and a well-thought-out battle plan. Several weeks before the election, the campaign manager should devise a clear schedule of the needs and activities of election day. He maps out clearly and in great detail what will be expected of precinct workers, poll watchers, and all others involved in the election day effort.

Centralization vs. Decentralization   The first aspect of election day organization to consider is whether to run a centralized or a de-centralized operation. There are advantages and disadvantages to both approaches that have to be weighed in light of the local situation.

Having your entire election day operation work out of the main cam-paign headquarters reduces the chances of duplication and increases the possibilities of tight, centralized control. Legal help can be made readily available, as can baby-sitting facilities and transporta-tion pools. On the other hand, the situation is often hectic, and enough telephones are usually not available for all the precinct cap-tains to make their phone calls to voters who have not yet voted.

In rural districts like the 2nd C.D. of California, which stretches 500 miles from the Oregon border down into southern California, decentralization is essential. In such a district, several headquarters must be set up. However, decentralization is sometimes a good idea in city districts as well. A decentralized operation increases familiarity with local conditions and neighborhood peculiarities, especially in areas with heavy ethnic concentrations. Someone helping the precinct pollwatcher can probably make the phone calls and arrange rides to the polls just as easily from his home as from central headquarters provided that he has been briefed on just what is expected of him and has a car handy. A decentralized approach also serves to curb somewhat that bane of all organizations-creeping bureaucratization. The fewer people around campaign headquarters during election day, the better the probability that workers with truly functional, assigned tasks will be able to carry them out.

In any type of decentralized operation, of course, it is essential that someone at the central headquarters be assigned the primary task of liaison and coordination with the local units, and being ready to supply them with services, such as legal aid, that could not be effectively provided at the local level.

Preparing for Election Day   In the week before election day, contact all your "sure" voters (1's) to remind them to vote and to find out if you can do anything (e.g., provide baby-sitters or car rides to the polling places) to make it easier for them to get to the polls. This is why the precinct leader must keep an up-to-date, inclusive hard card file. Such a file makes much easier the task of selecting every voter in the precinct with a good probability of voting for his candidate. About a week before the election, all precinct leaders should gather at the campaign headquarters to estimate the vote in their precincts and to present a general political intelligence report on their precinct to the campaign manager. All these efforts result in effective voter mobilization on election day.

Election Day Tactics   Election day is the culmination of all the hard work and effort of the preceding months. So that these efforts will pay off, set up a well-organized schedule for election day. Make sure that baby-sitting services and transportation are readily available.

Pollwatching   See that every precinct is manned by pollwatchers and challengers who have been carefully instructed in local election laws and the valid reasons for challenging voters. It is relatively simple to prevent an unqualified person from voting, and nearly impossible to invalidate his ballot once it has been cast.

Fraud, although not prevalent, is not unheard-of. It is likely to be a problem primarily in areas of overwhelming one-party domination where election board judges and workers of both parties are hard to find. To ensure the integrity of the polls:

1. Be at the polling place when the machines are opened to make sure all the numbers are set a zero.
2. If a machine becomes jammed, call the election board (immediately) and be sure to get names, addresses, and telephone numbers from the voters then in the polling place.

3. Keep your own tally of the number of people who cast ballots.

4. Have a pollwatcher present at all time to prevent opposition voters from running up the total by casting multiple ballots.

5. Pay careful attention when the numbers are transcribed from the machine to the tally sheet.

Fraud is much more likely to occur when paper ballots are used. The greater opportunity for fraud comes during the count. Be there before the polls close for the count, and stay until the tally sheets are turned in. Watch for deliberate attempts to spoil ballots, to illegally invalidate them, or simply to throw them away. One of Senator Birch Bayh's campaign managers in Indiana tells how a flashlight saved the Senator 50 votes in a rural district. An overzealous opposition election judge was simply slipping the ballots he didn't like out an open window. Aided by a flashlight, the Bayh forces were able to retrieve the lost ballots from a nearby cornfield. Fraud is seldom so blatant, and it is probably less prevalent than many people believe. It can be eliminated almost entirely by alert and knowledgeable election day work.

Pulling Out the Vote The presence of a pollwatcher is in itself a major deterrent to fraud. The election day worker need devote little time to legal and technical problems. His major task is to bring his candidate's supporters to the polls. Each precinct leader compiles a list, in triplicate, of all voters who, on the basis of canvassing information, appear to support his candidate. Each pollwatcher receives the list for his election districts and checks off the voters as they come to vote. At intervals six, four, and two hours before the polls close, a runner collects the lists and takes them to campaign headquarters, where a telephone crew calls voters whose names haven't been checked off, reminds them to vote, and asks if they need assistance in getting to the polls.

Challenging Challenging and pulling have top priority on election day, but if manpower is plentiful, last-minute electioneering may have an impact on voters who are still undecided. State laws closely limit the activities permitted in the vicinity of the polls. Electioneering is usually prohibited within 100 feet of the entrance to the polling place. Outside these limits, most voters can be handed a last-minute propaganda message to read on their way in. This is often a palm card showing the candidate's name on the ballot and a short, pointed message recalling the major themes and motifs of previously distributed brochures. Handouts at factory gates (if factory workers can be counted upon for your candidate) and at commuter and subway stations reminding people that the polls are still open, sound trucks in the districts which canvassing has shown to be most firmly committed to your side, and similar last-minute devices may also prove very worthwhile in an off-year, low-interest election.

By noon on election day only a very small proportion of the vote will have been cast, yet many candidates essentially end their campaigns the day before. We strongly suggest that media efforts--particularly on radio and in morning newspapers--be continued at least until midday on the day of decision. Useful as these last-minute reminders may prove, they should not siphon off manpower from work at the polls. Each pollwatcher can be expected to bring anywhere from two to 10 forgetful supporters to the voting booth. Few media appeals, sounds trucks, or leaflets can offer that kind of payoff.

If an effective, well-organized program has been employed and your candidate did not start the race hopelessly behind, election night can be a gratifying experience. Downcast faces, dark mutterings about "ballot stuffing" and "stealing votes" can be replaced by smiling workers congratulating each other on carrying out an efficient campaign that led to a tremendous victory.

5
Money, Propaganda, Polls, and Research

One of the most depressing signts in politics is the headquarters of
a defeated candidate on the day after the election. The posters and
decorations that looked so impressive the day before are tacky and
poorly placed. The unused flyers and brochures have lost their zip.
Boxes of buttons and bumper stickers have become worthless junk.

Every candidate and every campaign manager should be forced to pore
through this rubble and sort it out with care. More vividly than anything we can say here, it would tell how much wasted effort and sheer
nonsense go into every campaign. Look at this stack of mimeographed
sheets--seven pages on the history of American involvement in Vietnam--
did anybody read it? What about these 8-by-10 glossy photographs of
our peerless leader that cost 34¢ each--what end did they serve? And--
oh, my God, look at this--3,000 paper coffee cups printed with the candidate's name: How we could have used the media time that the price of
these cups would have bought!

Gimmicks can be useful in a campaign. So can research. Glossy
photographs may even have a place. But the key work in any campaign,
as it is now in our politics, is priorities. Where do you spend your
money? How do you use your time and available resources? The answers
to these questions are by and large beyond the range of most volunteers:
if the candidate and his immediate advisers have not set these schedules
of priorities long before volunteers are called, the campaign may already be beyond salvation. Beyond registration drives, beyond canvassing, and beyond election day activities, however, volunteers can
play a number of roles. Among them are fund-raising, leafleting, polling, and research.

FUND-RAISING

Every two years, the staunchest Congressional proponents of law
and order are flagrant violators of state and federal laws on campaign
finances. So are most other candidates. Under federal law, no candidate for the Senate may spend more than $25,000 on his campaign, no
candidate for the House more than $5,000. "I dearsay," said Repre-
sentative James C. Wright of Texas before the House Administration
Committee in 1966, "there is not a member of Congress, myself included,
who has not knowingly evaded (this law) in one way or another." Ten
one-minute spots on TV will usually cost more than the $5,000 allowed

to candidates for the House. One direct mailing to all registered Democrats in Connecticut would cost twice the amount permitted a candidate for the Senate. In a competitive House district, $30,00 is a low-budget campaign. In a large state like California or New York, million-dollar Senatorial races are not unusual.

Most of this money is used to by exposures. A glance at the stories in a typical newspaper will show why such expenditure is necessary. The amount of news space devoted to Congressional campaigns is literally too small to measure. Between September and November, the chances are that a local paper will devote more column inches to Charlie Brown and Little Orphan' Annie than to the candidates for Congress in the district. Unless he pays for it himself, a candidate's chances for getting on the prime-time TV are about as good as his chances of being elected Miss America. If such exposure cannot be bought, it must be gained in some other way. And, as we saw in the chapter on canvassing, name-recognition and exposure are directly related to a candidate's chances of electoral success. Even the most attractive candidate can be written off if he has no means of taking his message to the people, nor will his key issues reach the public.

The Volunteer's Role There are two ways in which volunteers can help bridge the money gap. One is through direct fund-raising campaigns. The other is by providing services that would otherwise have to be paid for out of the campaign budget.

There are thousands of ways to raise money. The best way is simply to ask for it. No gimmick is more effective than peer-group contact. If your target is a millionaire, the approach should be made by a fellow millionaire. Students should put the screws on fellow students; professors, on professors. And don't just ask for money--name the amount you want. If a candidate is worth your spending time on his campaign, surely he is worth more than 50¢ or a dollar from someone who shares your views and knows who you are. There is no substitute for the direct approach. Most people would prefer to give $10 outright than pay that amount for a rubber-chicken dinner and three hours of speeches.

There is no substitute for big money. Some people, with a flick of the pen, can give more money in a few seconds than 100 volunteers can collect in a week. Small contributions, however, are important for ideological reasons and because they buy commitment as well as goods and services. Every individual who makes a contribution, no matter how small, has bought a share of the campaign. On election day the chances are good that campaign donors will back their investments with votes. In the 1950s and early 1960s the Democratic party ran "Dollars for Democrats" drives that were highly effective from both points of view. Whether or not they will prove effective in the 1970s is problematic. Now there are so many groups, from the Heart Association to Jehovah's Witnesses, who have adopted the technique of door-to-door solicitation of small contributions that the average householder has built up elaborate and effective means of defense against solicitation.

Door-to-Door Fund-Raising The question of whether door-to door campaigns for donations are worthwhile is essentially a question of priorities. Suppose that a single canvasser could contact 50 households in a day. If he spent his time talking about candidates and issues, that time would mean 50 guaranteed exposures per day. If he spent that same time collecting money, could he produce enough to guarantee the equivalent exposure through the radio or television? Consider, in answering this question, that the average American is estimated to have been exposed to between 1,500 and 1,800 advertising messages a day.

Reaching the Contributor How do you reach the small contributor? In New York City, Mayor Lindsay's 1969 campaign averaged $1,000 a day from card tables set up on busy sidewalks. Selling buttons, or passing cans at state fairs or carnivals where people have loose change in their pockets, can be productive, too. Direct mailings, particularly those aimed at specific target groups--e.g., a doctor writing to his fellow doctors--should be tried, but largely as a last resort. Those in the profession of direct mail campaigns consider 3% returns as excellent. Still, every campaign should seriously attempt to set up special groups like Lawyers for Jones, Professors for Jones, etc., to channel publicity and raise money on a peer-group level. Even with these special committees, however, face-to-face contacts are best, phone calls second most effective, and mail solicitations come in a distant third.

Some fund-raising techniques can and should be organized outside of the campaign office. One of the most effective of these techniques has been the antiwar petition. In the aftermath of Cambodia and Kent State, a mass meeting at the University of Rochester developed the idea of circulating a nationwide petition designed both to express opposition to the war and to raise money for the cause of peace. The petition reads: "We ask the United States Congress to assert its constitutional powers in matters of war and peace, to condemn our recent invasion of Cambodia, and to require the President to bring our troops home. We wish no further military involvement in Indochina." Individuals are asked to sign the petition and to contribute 50¢ or more to buy media space and time for antiwar messages. In Rochester alone, for example, canvassers obtained more than 70,000 signatures and nearly $40,000 in about ten days of canvassing.

The National Petition Committee does not wish to become too closely linked to specific Congressional campaigns. It might be unwise for some candidates to become too closely linked to the pedition. The post-election poll reported in Chapter 2 showed that almost one-fourth of peace candidate Kaden's support came from people who favor the war. But there is no reason why the local branches of the National Petition Committee and various peace candidates cannot work out mutually useful agreements. Petition funds could be divided between the two groups. Petition lists could be supplied to campaign headquarters. And volunteers from both groups could be exchanged, as the demand for workers varies throughout a campaign. The National Petition Committee, moreover, has prepared some highly effective TV spots on the war which leave space at the end for a pitch from groups endorsing local candidates.

Whatever gimmicks are in use to raise money, there are never enough of them. Every campaign must develop its own special techniques for raising funds. Of all areas of campaign strategy, this is one of the most difficult about which to generalize. In one district, art shows in which local artists contribute 30% of the purchase price of their work to the campaign fund may be fabulously successful. In other districts, they might be utter disasters.

We can generally advise:

1. Direct solicitation on a face-to-face, peer-group basis is best.
2. The best method of soliciting small contributions is one that gives the contributor a feeling of having invested something in the campaign.
3. To encourage peer-group solicitation, special groups such as Lawyers for Jones should be established.
4. Contributions in kind can be an important adjunct to a volunteer effort. Room and board for out-of-town canvassers, casseroles for fund-raising dinners, and office space and equipment for headquarters can all be donated directly. A volunteer campaign can learn to live off the land.
5. Door-to-door solicitations run the risk of alienating oversolicited citizens and may not be an effective use of manpower. But they have the potential of substantially broadening both the financial and the volunteer bases of the campaign.
6. Congressional campaign committees should take full advantage of the fund-raising potential of other events and groups, from state fairs to the National Petition Campaign.

<u>When</u> <u>Volunteers</u> <u>Should</u> <u>Raise</u> <u>Money</u> A major cause of divorce in the United States is arguments over money. It is also a major cause of dispute within political campaigns. With the stock market down and unemployment up, this is a tough year for raising money. And there are no magic formulas. Should you charge for buttons and bumper stickers? Should you hold a $100-a-plate-dinner--or, for that matter, a $2-a-plate dinner from the local carry-out? We can only suggest this basic guideline: Don't use volunteer efforts for fund-raising if their efforts elsewhere would produce more candidate exposure than the expected monetary returns could buy.

Some kinds of volunteer effort can be used to offset a campaign's lack of funds. If yard signs have not been outlawed in your state, they are almost as effective as billboards. Like bumper stickers, they indicate a personal commitment while comveying a message. Because they have this personal touch, many volunteer activities--especially those run by natives of the district--are highly effective. There is no substitute for flesh-and-blood contact with the candidate, but a personal visit from one of his workers runs a close second. Television is effective because it gives a sense of contact: the viewer both sees and hears the candidate and his message. Some of this effect can be achieved through brochures with a high visual impact. No brochure should have more than two or three hundred words of text, but brevity is particularly important if leaflets are to be passed out in the street. Such gimmicks as balloons and combs imprinted with the candidates name are probably a waste of money.

<u>Other</u> <u>Volunteer</u> <u>Jobs</u> Again, let us emphasize that there is no sub-
stitute for effective face-to-face contact. Many volunteers, however,
do not make effective canvassers. What do you do with junior-high-
school students, those who are nervous about going from door to door,
and those who simply cannot be trusted with the job? The first rule
for dealing with such volunteers is never to turn them away. Every campaign headquarters should always have work available for those who
wish to do it--even if it means copying lists of names that will later
be thrown away. Such volunteers can be used to offset the costs of
direct mail by hand-delivering letters and brochures (warning: it is
illegal to put anything but the United States mail in a mailbox). They
can be sent to shopping centers to place bumper stickers on the cars
of those who give their consent. They can do the preliminary research
for canvassing drives. They can sort and file completed hard cards.
They can stuff envelopes. They can baby-sit for housewives out canvassing their districts. Any activities such as these which can be
performed free of charge are, literally, money in the bank.

PROPAGANDA

How should the money be spent? What about billboards? Bumper
stickers? Buttons? Golf tees? Mailings? Balloons? Headquarters?
Brochures? Television? Radio? Newspapers? Paid workers? Polls?
Professional consultants? Posters?

Every campaign manager and every candidate has his own favorite
answers to these questions. There are no scientific surveys which provide meaningful guidelines. Most candidates do everything they can
afford. A lot of money is spent on ego satisfaction. Wouldn't you be
thrilled to see your name on a bumper sticker? Or how about a big
picture of yourself smiling down on the passersby on Main Street? What
a disaster if all of a sudden your opponent is on radio and you aren't!
He had ten one-minute spots on TV. Where were you?

<u>Candidate</u> <u>Exposure</u> Particularly for nonincumbents, name recognition
is vital. It is helpful if that recognition is coupled with an image.
In 1970 the image of change, of a new politics, is a plus in most areas.
It is also psychologically useful, to voters and particularly to workers
in the campaign, to convey an image of growing support and enthusiasm.
Whatever methods a candidate used to get his name and message to the
voter, he is working in a highly competitive arena. He is competing
not just with other candidates but with cigarettes, soaps, hotels, and
markets.

Every professional campaign consultant has his own favorite device
for successfully competing for voter attention. Stephen Shaddegg pre-
fers window decals, timed to appear only in the final weeks of the campaign, that create an image of growing support. Others will put $4 of
every $5 into TV. The choice will depend largely on the location of
the district and the nature of the campaign. It is pointless for a
candidate in Chicago to pay the TV rates for the entire Chicago area
in order to reach one small district within it. TV ads run before
10:00 P.M. cost more and are likely to reach as many children as voters.
Bumper stickers are of little use in Manhattan, though shopping bags
may serve in their stead.

38

Strategy of Exposure Much valuable time can be wasted in arguing the technical details of candidate exposure. It really doesn't matter much whether the bumper stickers are purple and green, or light white and dark black. It matters quite a bit that all candidate-exposure devices be coordinated into a coherent strategy. This strategic plan has two elements. First is timing. Plan from election day backward. The overall pattern is one of growing exposure through the four weeks before the elections. The major saturation comes in the week before the election. Coordinate minor buildups with other campaign events. Before a town is canvassed, lay the groundwork with a media barrage. Then, hopefully, the voter will have some vague idea of whom the canvasser is talking about. Follow up a major newsbreak immediately with reinforcing ads. If the candidate's statement on Indian affairs gets front-page treatment, for example, repeat and reinforce the theme in follow-up ads.

The second important element in the strategy of candidate exposure is the sounding of a consistent and coherent theme. Emphasize clear contrasts with the opposition. Let visual images, type styles, and literature format, as well as issues, play up this contrast. See that consistent patterns, either visual or thematic, link all separate brochures and media into an identifiable whole. Most important, be brief. Finally, plan all candidate exposure operations from the perspective of the voter, not of the campaign. Candidate exposure is not a theoretical problem. First and most important, the voter needs to know who is running for what office and why it is important to him. If necessary, design specific brochures for specific audiences. Knowing how to prepare these pamphlets and where to use them is the key to success. A bad brochure may be worse than none at all.

POLLING

In planning a campaign, few devices are more useful than public opinion polls. What is a poll for? How can nonprofessionals contribute to such surveys?

Many people think that the most important function of a poll is to find out who is ahead at a certain juncture in the race. From the candidate's point of view, this is its least important function. The purpose of a sample survey is to locate the issues which certain groups of voters think are the most important. Then voter attitudes toward these issues may be assessed comparatively. The final poll analysis tells the best ways of exploiting public attitudes toward the candidate and his platform.

What Is a Poll? A poll is simply a device for finding out from a relatively small sample of the population how the population as a whole is likely to react to certain stimuli. Badly done, a poll can be worse than useless. Properly done, however, it can provide a crucial supplement to the opinions of the campaign staff, which are usually unrepresentative. The hunches and guesses of activists and volunteers are often the worst possible guides to district opinion. All too often, the particular set of issues that seems most important to campaign volunteers is not the one that matters most to the electorate in a particular district. For example, the Vietnam war may be the overriding concern of students working for a Congressional candidate. But if the price of food is worrying housewives, it would be folly not to be aware of this fact and take account of it.

Regular political activists, as well as amateur volunteers, may also be out of step with what the electorate thinks are important issues. The "regulars" may feel the pressures of the most active of the constituents. A candidate's staff may be subtly influenced by spokesmen for pressure groups. Their view of the total electorate's opinion on a certain issue may have been swayed by a strongly expressed minority view in the district.

<u>Who</u> <u>Is</u> <u>Polled</u>? We have been talking about the electorate as a whole. But the candidate must be able to break up his electorate so that he is dealing with groups of voters, with voters at precinct levels. A public opinion survey can help volunteers themselves to become better informed about the electorate with whom they are going to be engaged. It can also help identify which areas of the Congressional district are likely to be favorable to the candidate and/or to his views on issues. This information will be useful in determining where student canvassers can be most effective.

Serious mistakes can be avoided through judicious use of information gathered in a public opinion survey. The Kaden campaign volunteers would have pulled many less Patten voters to the polls if they had known in advance where Patten's strength was concentrated. The issues that are important in one part of a Congressman's district may not be important in another part.

Any survey of public opinion must have a well-chosen sample. A poll surveys only a small part of the electorate. The larger the sample, the more costly the poll, whether it is done door-to-door, by telephone, or through the mails. The sample must accurately reflect the proportion of the various groups in the constituency. A number of factors come into play in selecting the sample: income, race, occupation, area of residence, religion, party affiliation, sex, age, ethnicity, propensity to vote. Any factor that is itself significant in electoral politics must be considered in drawing up a sample.

<u>Using</u> <u>a</u> <u>Professional</u> <u>Pollster</u> Having a properly weighted sample is so important that professional advice and help must be sought here. The professional pollster must be told what the campaign needs to know before a questionnaire is drawn up. It may be decided to sample the districts all at once. Or an opinion sample on one specific issue may be conducted within one age, income, or ethnic group. Obviously, principal characteristics of the target group must be taken into account in order for the sample to be conducted successfully.

University students often have access to people who know sampling procedures and can construct questionnaires. Major public opinion survey groups exist, for example, at the University of Chicago and the University of Michigan. Many social scientists do opinion surveys as part of their scholarly work. Many students have also done survey analysis. Thus the volunteers may themselves have expertise here.

But before proceeding with a public opinion survey, volunteers had better be sure that those claiming to be experts do know what they are about. Sometimes persons who work for a professional polling agency will be willing to help out on an individual basis.

Volunteer Pollsters Many candidates want to sponsor their own polls, but cannot afford the costs involved. If candidates do not have access to free advice from professionals, they may still benefit from inexpensive interviewing provided by volunteers. Amateur interviewing can, and often does, produce inaccurate results. But it need not. This is especially true when telephone interviews are being considered. Volunteer interviewers can help candidates. They can even assess their own role in a campaign. Volunteers can man telephones or distribute questionnaires. They can even do person-to-person interviewing. But all this is possible only if the volunteers are properly trained and instructed.

In the Movement for a New Congress's post-election poll on the impact of student canvassing for Lew Kaden in New Jersey, which was analyzed in Chapter 2, reaearchers in the Movement office told professional pollsters in Princeton what they wanted to learn from the poll. The professionals drew up the sample and analyzed the results, assisted by a Movement researcher whom we wished to train in poll analysis. But the poll was completely administered through phone banks at Movement headquarters. The volunteer interviewers doing the phoning met to be instructed in the use of the questionnaire. They were told how to introduce themselves, how to explain their purpose, how long to make the conversation, and how to record answers on the questionnaire sheet.

If a telephone poll is being done, it is important to have a good-sized bank of phones in one central place. At least seven or eight are needed. Morale drops when volunteers do a few calls and get refusals or no answer. Having several volunteers working together on the phones helps to keep spirits up. Also, someone with interview experience should be around the phone bank to check on the interviewers.

The Movement's New Jersey poll aimed at a 500-voter sample. We were prepared to have fewer. But we have to complete whole groups within the sample so that the sample results would not be skewed. For example, if calls are made during the day, a disproportionate number of women will be reached at home. Or responses may be higher in one residential area than another. It is necessary to complete packets of numbers as they were made up by the person drawing up the sample, if the sample results are to be at all accurate.

Analyzing and Using the Results After the poll is carried out, competent people must code responses and analyze the questionnaire answers. At this stage volunteers can at least save money by providing phones and manning them. Again, the volunteers must be properly trained in the art of follow-up interviewing and in correlating results.

The Movement poll in Middlesex County took place after the election. Don't do a post-election poll--or any poll, for that matter--if you foresee no use for the information. Our purpose is this case was to reach conclusions about the potential effect of student canvassers on future campaigns in this and other districts. We wanted to know specifically how student volunteers were received by prospective voters and how students affected voting patterns in the places they canvassed. The results were discussed at length with campaign organizers for Kaden, who were able to test their own views against the opinion survey results.

A final word of advice. It is likely that other organizations, including professional pollsters like Gallup and Harris, have already done opinion surveys on at least some of the issues that concern you. Try to find out in advance what kinds of results have already been obtained. For example, nationwide work has been done on the reception of students in campaigns and on attitudes toward the Vietnam war by age and ethnic group. Surveys have probably been done on candidates with positions that are similar to those of the candidate you are working for.

Even if your findings are strikingly different from previous ones, your poll analysis may accurately reflect public opinion in your district or state. You should, however, look very carefully at your results if they seem to be atypical. These variant results are often the most interesting ones, but it is especially important to be sure that they are correct. It is here that adjustments in your particular campaign may have to be made. Unique factors in your constituency, or factors pertaining to your candidate, may require special attention. A result that was unexpected may also be showing a trend effect. Remember, polls give you a picture of public opinion at a particular point in time. Attitudes are always in flux, and past polls may not accurately reflect public opinion now—another reason for doing comparisons with earlier polls. Or you can compare your results with results in another state or district. It is very important, but also difficult, to be able to pinpoint changes in public opinion and to isolate the events that led to these changes.

RESEARCH

Nine of every ten volunteers will ask to do research. If allowed to go their own way, they will produce reams of detailed reports on topics ranging from the ABM to the price of eggs. During his brother's 1960 campaign for the presidency, Robert Kennedy developed a stock answer for those who came to him with offers to solve the problems of disarmament, poverty, and race relations: "Fine," Kennedy would say, "but can you lick stamps?" Licking stamps may be less fun, but it often produces more votes than much of the research effort that is likely to go into a campaign.

What Is Useful Research We do not mean to downgrade the importance of good research: few parts of the campaign are more important. What must be stressed is that all research operations must be relevant to the major objective: winning the election. One of the most important areas of research is the development of detailed profiles of the district. Polls, in this sense, are a fact of research. Indeed, a good poll can be conducted only on the basis of good preliminary research that locates major subgroups of the population and defines key issues and image problems.

<u>Practical</u> <u>Research</u> The research staff works in close harmony with
the rest of the campaign. It provides those working on registration
with detailed district-by-district analyses of registration patterns,
past voting behavior, and population characteristics. It provides canvassers with material on the kinds of attitudes they are likely to find
in particular kinds of districts. It provides the publicity department
with short, pithy statements on major issues. And it carefully monitors
and evaluates the record, background, and campaign of the opponent.

The research team must work closely with scheduling and campaigning
to supply the background on where to go and what to say. Such seemingly trivial questions as what gate factory workers use, what time the
candidate can best arrive at a dinner to avoid having to sit and listen
to the other speakers, and what times are best for appearances at shopping centers can do much to conserve the most valuable resource of the
campaign: the candidate himself.

<u>Issue</u> <u>Research</u> Issue research can be divided into three catego-
ries. First, background briefing sessions with the candidate and other
major figures in the campaign should be scheduled at least once a week.
The purpose of these sessions is not simply to inform the candidate
but also to keep research abreast of feedback from other campaign efforts.
What kinds of questions are people asking during campaign appearances?
What are the canvassers finding out about voters' attitudes? How well
are the brochures being received? Briefing sessions must begin very
early in the campaign and cover a wide range of issues. Voters may not
be well-informed themselves, but they most certainly expect their politicians to be versed in current issues.

Second, research must be able to provide background papers on a
selected range of key issues. A candidate must obviously be prepared
to discuss the war in Vietnam, inflation, and similar issues of uni-
versal concern. Research must not, however, overlook issues of spe-
cialized concern to the district and to key subgroups within it. This
effort may in fact be more important. In most cases, candidates have
already developed their positions on the war and similar issues. Research can add little beyond frills and statistics, and these are likely
to be beyond the competence or concern of most voters. The one target
group for which such research might be useful is the volunteers. It
is important that they know the candidate's positions, and they are
likely to be well enough informed to use detailed analyses. Long
issue statements, however, are best saved for internal distribution.

While the research team is preparing background papers for the campaign staff, it must also be keeping abreast of the opposition. The
Congressional records of most incumbents contain numerous weak spots
that can be exploited in the campaign: poor attendance, bad votes or
crucial absences, and foolish statements on the floor make good targets
for campaign jibes.

The third key function of research is to prepare policy statements
for use in brochures, speeches, and press releases. Most important
are short statements on key issues. Ironically, many candidates will
put in long hours working over a speech to be delivered before 75 Rotarians (most of whom have already made up their minds) and then turn
around and give a radio broadcaster an uninformed, off-the-cuff state-

ment that will be heard by 25,000. Every candidate should have committed to memory a short statement in answer to questions on any major issues that may arise. Such short statements are also the stuff of brochures, press releases, and briefings for volunteers.

PUTTING IT ALL TOGETHER

One of the most difficult problems in a volunteer organization is the coordination and control of work. A campaign is not the place to "do your own thing." Teamwork is essential, and priority schedules must be observed. Not everyone can do research; some must lick stamps. No canvasser, no matter how many previous campaigns he has worked in, should go out into the field without a thorough briefing. No one at any stage or in any facet of the campaign should lose sight of the overall goal of winning at least 50% plus one of the votes cast.

Let us end this section, as we began, with a post-election visit to campaign headquarters, in this case the base of a victorious effort. Here, perhaps, are the same wasted coffee cups--looking a little better perhaps with the remains of victory champagne glistening in the bottom, but still a waste of resources. Here are no leftover piles of literature--research and publicity were well enough coordinated to get all pieces of literature delivered. There are no unusable photographs, no senseless gimmicks, priorities having been carefully set and adhered to.

Here, most important, is the victorious candidate. Will his record in Washington live up to expectations? Will he return for his next campaign strengthened by his experiences or wearied and frustrated by institutions that are too slow to respond and by problems that yeild no easy solutions?

And here too is the team that put him in office. Where do they go from here?

6
Keeping
the Movement Alive

The job is not finished once election day has passed. Not only must preparations begin for the next election, but some steps must be taken to follow through on the work already begun. In Washington, the real voice of the American people sounds strangely muted. The politician as campaigner and the politican as office holder are different animals. But if constituents are to keep check on their representatives, they must know what they are talking about, how they can best approach the office holder, and how they can hold him accountable for his actions.

MONITORING CONGRESS

How do you keep informed about what your Congressman is doing? Mailings from the Congressman's office must be taken with a grain of salt. They are political propaganda intended not to portray accurately the member's stand on a wide spectrum of issues but only to help his image with the voters.

Local newspapers seldom devote much space to a Congressman's Washington activities, and therefore the political activist should be aware of the primary sources of information on Congressmen, most of which are available in University or public libraries. A Congressman's biography and committee assignments can be found in the Congressional Directory. His record on roll-call votes is easily obtainable; two excellent publications, Congressional Quarterly and National Journal, publish weekly reports on all the activities in Congress, including listings of all roll-call votes. Their simpler format and the condensed synopses presented for each vote make them sources more useful than the official one, the Congressional Record. Listings of how Senators and Representatives voted on major issues, such as the Cooper-Church Amendment, are usually printed in the following day's edition of the Washington Post, which most libraries carry.

The new reorganization of the House of Representatives may eliminate a procedure that allows some members to cast "secret" votes on many crucial issues. Most voting in the House is now done while it sits as the Committee of the Whole House on the State of the Union, a parliamentary device intended to speed up and make less formal the House's business by reducing from 218 to 100 the number of members needed to constitute a quorum. While the House is sitting as the Committee of the Whole, issues are settled by voice votes, standing divisions, or

teller votes, in which members are counted but not individually recorded. It is very difficult to get an accurate list of how members
vote on tellers, and some members are thus able to vote in ways that
would displease their constituents were their votes known. Reformers
hope to do away with such secret votes by instituting record teller
votes whereby clerks would record each member's vote, which would then
be reported in the <u>Congressional</u> <u>Record</u>.

MAKING YOUR CONGRESSMAN MORE EFFECTIVE

Unlike Senators, members of the House of Representatives have very
little staff assistance available for legislative work. Most of the
time and energy of the Washington office must go to administrative
problems, answering the mail, responding to constituents' requests for
help and information, and carrying out similar nonlegislative tasks.
Beyond the range of issues dealt with by the committees to which he
is assigned, the typical member simply lacks the resources seriously
to consider new programs, much less to innovate them. The pressures
of time are so great, moreover, that he has little opportunity to reflect on the larger questions of priorities, trends, and issue development. Administrative agencies, lobbies, and colleagues can be counted
upon to fill a part of this void, but concerned constituent groups
might also be able to perform valuable services.

<u>Using</u> <u>Local</u> <u>Sources</u> It is striking how rapidly campaign organi-
zations dissolve. What happens to the research done during the campaign? Who is there to follow it up and turn campaign promises into
specific proposals for legislative action? Citizens in every Congressional district have valuable knowledge: knowledge of issues both
local and national which Congressmen could use. Yet the organizational
vehicles for bringing Congressmen and their informational needs together with these sources of advice and information cease to exist
once a campaign ends. Perhaps candidates should give serious consideration to establishing, out of their campaign operations, continuing
advisory bodies or "kitchen cabinets" to maintain these links. Not
only could such boards make the member more effective in the House,
they could also contribute substantially to his possibilities for reelection two years later when his record in Washington becomes a campaign issue.

Even for defeated candidates, institutions analagous to the British
"shadow cabinet" might be set up to continuously monitor and comment
upon the work of the victorious opponent. By the time a newly elected
Congressman takes office in January, his next campaign is only 18 months
away, and it is never too early to begin.

<u>Exchanging</u> <u>Ideas</u> Information is only one of the many services that
constituency groups can provide a Congressman. Congressmen should be
encouraged frequently to try out their ideas and reflect on their experiences before sympathetic but detached audiences. Yet for many
members such audiences are not easy to find. The contours of a Congressman's visits to his district are shaped by the organizations that
can provide him with audiences large enough to merit his time. His
impressions of constituency opinion are likely to be shaped by the best
organized of his constituents: Chambers of Commerce, Elks, Rotarians,
Veteran's groups, and so on. Special interest groups fill a very large

part of his contact time. From his perspective there will be many silent majorities and minorities who conbributed to his campaign and then disappeared from view. Volunteer activists can serve an important role as supplementary eyes and ears in the district. Intelligence on emerging issues of local importance or on key political developments can be very useful.

LOBBYING

The astonishing invasion of Cambodia stirred thousands of citizens to go to Washington in the spring of 1970 to urge their Congressman to restrict this widening of the war. The earliest efforts were hit-or-miss, spur-of-the-moment attempts, but within weeks, well-organized lobbying efforts began to take place on Capitol Hill. For example, the Academic and Professional Alliance for a Responsible Congress re-cruited, briefed, and arranged appointments for delegations of business-men, professors, lawyers, doctors, and other groups to press the case for peace with their Representatives and Senators. These well-planned visits undoubtedly contributed to the surprisingly large Senate vote for the Cooper-Church and Hatfield-McGovern amendments.

Without such planning, however, lobbying can be more frustrating than productive. It would be hard to imagine another political activity in which so many have invested so much time and energy to get so little return. What many amateur lobbyists tend to forget is that members of Congress have minds of their own, and are, as part of their job, sur-prisingly well-informed about the major issues of the day.

If certain elementary ground rules are kept in mind, lobbying can tip the balance of a closely divided contest. If poorly planned, and poorly executed, lobbying can actually do harm to a good cause. Here are some useful tips.[1]

First of all, lobby only your own Congressman. Members could not care less about people who cannot vote for or against them. If you are from his district, and especially if you are identified with some electoral organization that actually puts workers into the field, you will probably get a respectful hearing.

<u>Know the Issues</u> This respect can disappear very quickly, however, if you display little knowledge of the member's publicly stated posi-tions on the issues, or if the legislation for which you are lobbying was voted on two months ago or will not be voted on until six months from now. Do your homework, and realize that Congress, particularly the House, is an institution that emphasizes division of labor and specialization. Do not expect a member of the Agriculture Committee to be terribly worried (or informed) about the Head Start program, or a member of Education and Labor to be very interested in farm subsidy programs. In the same vein, a constituent who, in a letter or visit, displays specialized expertise on some particular problem which is of interest to the Congressman will be respected and receive a good hear-ing. If you are going to Washington to talk about the war, check in first with Operation Pursestrings, the Continuing Presence in Washing-ton, the National Committee for a Sane Nuclear Policy, or similar groups to obtain a thorough briefing on both the issues at hand and the posi-tion of the member or members you plan to contact. Before you go home, check back in with these groups so that others may later benefit from

your experiences.

All studies of lobbying show that it is most effective when carried out as a reinforcement rather than a conversion function. A member can feel much more secure in taking positions when he knows, or has been led to believe, that substantial support for his position exists among the political elites of his district. Such selective lobbying can also sometimes raise an issue from low to high visibility in the eyes of a Congressman. A Congressman or Senator who is known to be leaning toward your position but is still sitting on the fence can sometimes be brought over by a well-organized lobbying effort. If he receives 1,000 well-written letters on the subject, he might be won over. On the other hand, nothing raises Congressional hackles quicker than massive form-letter write-in campaigns in which 5,000 of the 10,000 letters are addressed, "Dear Congressman Write in Name of Your Representative Here." For some reason, most Congressmen perceive such letters as the product of weak minds and accordingly assign them to the circular file.

Such organizations as the Continuing Presence in Washington can be most effective when directed at specific targets, such as the Cooper-Church and Hatfield-McGovern amendments. However, even such specifically oriented groups as these encounter terrific difficulties when legislation shifts from the Senate to the House and the number of "undecided" members to be lobbied jumps from 15-20 quite identifiable Senators to 80-100 essentially unknown Congressmen. A substantial army of volunteers is needed even to keep track of the many shades and nuances of House opinion and of shifts in voting blocs and alliances within so large and unwieldy a body. It is particularly easy in the House to be "booby-trapped" by technicalities in rules and procedures. Careful organization is a prerequisite of effective lobbying on a major issue.

Using Other Lobbyists Both in Washington and at the grass roots, a technique that is often effective is to lobby existing organizations like the AFL-CIO, trade associations, or professional societies, in order to get them to put their resources (which are usually better organized) to work on doing the actual lobbying in Washington. This is much less expensive and may result in the formation of local alliances that can be very worthwhile in future elections. The Continuing Presence in Washington has had considerable success in using college alumni contacts as entrees into existing organizations within Congressional districts throughout the country.

Is Lobbying Worthwhile? Lobbying and electoral activity are two sides of the same coin. The Congressman pays more attention to lobbyists from his constituency if he knows that new forces are stirring back home in the district. Then, after the election, he is more likely to listen to lobbyists who were manning the barricades when it counted-- in the election. Much of the time spent in lobbying activities, particularly when it is random and ill-coordinated, could be spent much more profitably in direct electoral action. Fifty students spending two hours in a rap session with some Congressman will probably have little effect on his views. Yet, if those 100 man hours were spent doing precinct work in his district, there would be a much high probability that he might move closer to your position, or even adopt it.

The effectiveness of a lobbying effort is frequently in inverse ratio to the national significance of the issue. Your letter on Cambodia is likely to be seen only as one of thousands on both sides of the question representing a rather biased sample of constituency opinion. A carefully considered discussion on a little discussed issue, or one of largely local concern, amy in itself be sufficient to produce action. Good lobbying is seen by Congressmen as a service: it provides information they could not otherwise get. Even this kind of lobbying, however, is most effective when it is backed by the potential promise of effective electoral activity.

The most effective lobbyist of all, most Congressmen will admit, is an informed and respected colleague. Thus, mobilizing those friendly to your cause is an important lobbying strategy. It depends, however, upon finding the right targets: those members who enjoy the greatest respect and prestige within the legislature.

POWER IN CONGRESS: THE "INSIDERS"

Who are the most powerful members? Obviously, committee chairmen, the Speaker of the House, the majority and minority leaders are important. Parallel to the formal structure of Congress is an informal power structure of highly respected Senators and Representatives. Both houses of Congress have, in addition to their formal rules, a set of informal rules or "folkways" about which considerable agreement exists.[2] There is a fairly high correlation between those members with the most internal influences and those who adopt this "insider's" role orientation.

The Outsider's Role Liberals exhibit a market tendency to adopt the alternative, the outsider's role. While this role may be more satisfying to the individual, in that it allows him to speak out on a wide range of issues, it also makes him a less effective legislator. In his classic article, "The Outsider in the Senate," Ralph Huitt comments that "the behavior associated with the Outsider may be functional for protest groups seeking a spokesman, (but) dysfunctional for protest groups seeking leverage inside the legislative body."[3]

Important decisions affecting the life chances of millions of Americans are made daily within the halls of Congress. Members who adopt the outsider role do so at the cost of relinquishing influence on these decisions. Unfortunately, those from highly competitive districts often feel that they must adopt the outsider's role in order to survive politically. Nicholas Masters has described "responsible" legislators, those, in other words, with the greatest influence, as men who:

> serve to enhance the prestige and importance of the body,... have respect for the legislative process,... understand and appreciate its formal and informal rules,... have the respect of their fellows,... don't try to manipulate every situation for personal advantage,... are willing to compromise,... have a moderate approach.[4]

In an analysis of why Carl Albert, the Majority Whip, overwhelmed the more externally well-known Richard Bolling for Majority Leader in

1962, references to Mr. Albert's role style were repeatedly mentioned. One interviewee described Albert's approach to his job:

> he developed quite a genius for knowing what people would do.... a service he performed that endeared him to people was that he was the kind of guy everybody could find.[5]

For these reasons, among others, Albert is the almost certain choice to succeed the retiring John McCormack as Speaker of the House.

In order to "know what people would do" and be a "guy everybody could find," members must spend inordinate amounts of time in the often dreary job of staying on the floor instead of attending to the mass of other business most Congressmen have. Mr. Albert prided himself in spending a greater proportion of his time on the floor of the House than any other member, where he was continually accessible to other members. Sticking to internal legislative business and eschewing speech-making, publicity tours, and so on is the way such men obtain the feel for the House's mores and temperament that is essential to an effective legislative leader.

The differing styles of Robert Kennedy and Edward Kennedy offer a good example of contrasting role behavior. Robert Kennedy failed to observe the usual apprenticeship period for freshman Senators and was continually speaking out on the principal issues of the day. He also was frequently absent and did little to cultivate internal influence in the Senate. On the other hand, his younger brother went along with the Senate's folkways. He waited the expected time before making a major speech. At the end of the day, he often dropped in on his chairman on the Judiciary Committee, James Eastland, to share a bourbon and branch water and discuss the day's legislative happenings. Such assiduous cultivation of the Senate's mores paid off when Kennedy was able to defeat a member of the Senate's establishment, Russell Long, for the Majority Whip position in 1969. Former Senator Wayne Morse, himself a prototypical outsider, attributed Kennedy's victory to the undisputed feeling in the Senate that he was a hard-working Senator who had a strong allegiance to the Senate as a body and respected its rules and traditions.

Liberal Outsiders   Why do so many liberals choose the outsider's role? Ideology is part of the answer: Congressional norms tend to have a conservative bias. Temperament is also a factor: those who wish to change the system can easily be discouraged by the slow pace of the legislative process. In many cases, however, liberals are ineffective because their constituents demand it. For the unsophisticated, the insider's role is difficult to appreciate.

Liberals and Committees   Another area of liberal weakness is in the committee structure of both houses. For years conservative southerners have maintained a disproportionate share of the chairmanships of major committees and important subcommittees. This control has not been accidental. Seniority is one of the principal informal rules of Congress. If a member stays on the same committee to which he was initially assigned and enjoys reasonably good health, he can expect to become chairman of the committee in 12 to 16 years.

In the past the southerners, under the leadership of the wily Judge Smith of Virginia, deliberately maneuvered to place at least one of their number on each committee and to keep him there, accruing valuable seniority. For instance, John McMillan, the chairman of the District of Columbia Committee, remained on that little-sought-after committee for over ten years watching liberals come and go until he became chairman. Since that time (1954) he has had enormous influence over the lives of District residents--many of whom were desperately in need of liberal-initiated social programs. Unfortunately liberals had fled the D.C. Committee for the greener pastures of Education and Labor or Banking and Currency, thereby abdicating control of the committee to conservatives. Better planning on the part of liberals during the initial assignment process and a greater willingness to remain on the less attractive committees would greatly increase the number of liberals in seniority positions on a wide range of committees. These seniority positions, in turn, serve as the principal power bases for members trying to develop initial influence.

It is important to remember that committee-based influences derive not only from committee chairmanships but also from important sub-committee chairmanships. An unanticipated byproduct of the reduction in the number of standing committees (from 48 to 19),[6] resulting from the Legislative Reorganization Act of 1946, has been growth in the number and importance of subcommittees. Richard Fenno has pointed out that any analyses of power in the House "which excludes the 123 subcommittees can be but caricatures of the (actual) influence patterns."[7]

Liberal Issues Within the Congress Should New Congress candidates achieve significant victories this fall, it is vital to the continuing success of the Movement that they be encouraged to use their power to maximum effect. They must be encouraged in particular to pay continuing attention to some of the less glamorous issues of structural and political reform. There will be an attack on the seniority system in the Democratic caucus. It should receive massive public backing. There will be leadership fights in both parties. The position of Majority Leader in the House should receive particular attention. The election of a reform-minded liberal like Morris Udall or James O'Hara would be a tremendous shot in the arm to progressive forces in the Democratic party. Candidates should be forced to commit themselves. Above all, liberal constituents should encourage their representatives to extend the power of the new politics into the halls of the New Congress.

FOLLOWING THROUGH IN THE DISTRICT

Politics is hard work. Tedious meetings and boring jobs are part of the package. These, however, are the prices of power. To those who persist, who are not political morning glories, the system is open for the taking. The time to begin is now. Campaign '72 has already begun.

1972 Is Now! A number of other campaigns taking place this year will have a bearing on the outcome in 1972. State legislatures elected this year will have the job of reapportionment to deal with in 1971. When the 1970 Census is completed, population shifts will result in some states losing Congressional representation at the expense of fast-growing areas in the Far West and South. All states that gain or lose seats must redistrict before 1972, and because of internal population shifts most others will have to reapportion in order to conform to the Supreme Court's one-man, one-vote guideline. Even under the rule of one-man, one-vote, the opportunities for gerrymandering are ever present and ever tempting.

The future balance of the next decade's Congressional delegations in states like California will be decided by what happens in races for the state legislature and the governor in 1970. Tomorrow's candidates for higher office will emerge from contests for minor positions today. Also at stake in 1970 are the political futures of men like Teddy Kennedy, Ed Muskie, and Ronald Reagan: can they win big and demonstrate the vote-getting power that could project them into the 1972 presidential campaign?

The answers to many of these questions will be decided in 1970. But few political decisions are irrevocable. If the energies mobilized now can be sustained, the heat will be on both the administration and the Congress to respond. If the forces pushing for change can demonstrate staying power as well as enthusiasm, the system will change.

The American party system is structured from the bottom up. There is no centralized control. That is why it is possible for Strom Thurmond and Jacob Javits both to consider themselves loyal Republicans, why James Eastland and George McGovern are both Democrats. If the locus of political power can be traced in our two parties it winds through the very smallest units--precinct and district captians, ward leaders and county chairmen--these are the men who run our political parties. Yet many districts have no leaders; no one is interested in running. Many others have figureheads who do not work and can be defeated easily. In 1963, thousands of these seemingly insignificant posts were won by hard-line conservatives who were looking ahead to 1964. It was their hard work that put such nonprimary states as Washington into the Goldwater column at the 1964 Republican convention. Similar efforts, starting now, can determine the outcome of the nominating process in 1972.

WORKING TOWARD A NEW POLITICS

Individual citizens can have an impact on the political process. To do so, they must be willing to work hard and to channel their efforts into effective forms of activity. Congress in an important part of our political system, but it is only a part. A New Congress alone cannot guarantee peace and a reordering of national priorities. Nor will the newly elected members in 1970 fulfill the bright hopes of their supporters unless they are given continuing motives for doing so. Only you can decide how much or how little of that support and that pressure will be brought to bear.

Resource Materials

THE 111 MOST MARGINAL HOUSE DISTRICTS

Listed below are those districts in which the incumbent's margin did not exceed 15 per cent. Listed separately are nine seats in which the retirement of the incumbent makes a formerly "safe" seat now a marginal one. The advantages of incumbency generally add about 5% to the expected margin in a typical district. With a good candidate and effective canvassing, a 15% margin is not insurmountable.

Marginality of districts as arrived at by strict statistical analysis must, of course, be complemented by the introduction of other relevant factors such as reapportionment and non-incumbency. The numbers after some member's names in the list below refer to such factors. The number code is as follows:

1. The incumbent is not seeking reelection because of retirement, primary defeat, etc.

2. The incumbent is in his first term.

3. Since 1968, reapportionment has helped the incumbent's chances for reelection.

4. Since 1968, reapportionment has hurt the incumbent's chances for reelection.

NOTE: A special case which does not fit any of the above categories is the new 29th District of New York. It contains parts of the old 29th and 35th districts and matches the two incumbents of those formerly safe districts, Daniel Button (R) and Samuel Stratton (D).

				1968 Vote	
State	CD	Incumbent	P	Incumbent	Challenger
North Dakota	2	Tom Kleppe 1	R	49.9%	48.7%
New Jersey	9	Henry Helstoski	D	49.8%	48.6%
New Mexico	2	Ed Foreman 2	R	50.5%	49.1%
New York	5	Allard K. Lowenstein 2,4	D	50.7%	49.3%
California	34	Richard T. Hanna	D	50.9%	49.1%
Wisconsin	1	Henry C. Schadeberg	R	50.9%	49.1%
Minnesota	7	Odin Langen	R	51.2%	48.8%
North Carolina	8	Earl B. Ruth 2	R	51.2%	48.8%
Louisiana	2	Hale Boggs 3	D	51.2%	48.8%
New York	28	Hamilton Fish, Jr.	R	48.1%	45.6%
California	17	Glenn M. Anderson 2	D	50.7%	48.1%
Indiana	4	E. Ross Adair	R	51.4%	48.6%
New York	16	John M. Murphy 4	D	48.8%	46.0%
Kansas	1	Keith G. Sebelius 2	R	51.5%	48.5%
New York	27	Martin B. McKneally 2	R	47.9%	44.9%
North Carolina	4	Nick Galifianakis	D	51.5%	48.5%
Pennsylvania	6	Gus Yatron	D	51.4%	47.5%
Ohio	23	William E. Minshall	R	52.0%	48.0%
Connecticut	4	Lowell P. Weicker, Jr. 1,2	R	51.4%	47.3%
Colorado	1	Byron G. Rogers	D	45.7%	41.5%
Colorado	3	Frank E. Evans	D	52.1%	47.9%
Indiana	3	John Brademas	D	52.2%	47.8%
Missouri	9	William L. Hungate 3	D	52.2%	47.8%
California	29	George E. Brown 1	D	52.3%	47.7%
North Carolina	5	Wilmer D. Mizell	R	52.4%	47.6%
Maryland	5	Lawrence J. Hogan 2	R	52.7%	47.3%
Florida	4	William V. Chappell 2	D	52.8%	47.2%
Maryland	6	J. Glenn Beall,Jr. 1,2	R	53.0%	47.0%
Iowa	1	Fred Schwengel	R	53.0%	47.0%
New Mexico	1	Manuel Lujan 2	R	52.8%	46.6%
Indiana	11	Andrew Jacobs, Jr.	D	53.1%	46.9%
Missouri	2	James W. Symington 3	D	53.2%	46.8%
Tennessee	5	Richard Fulton	D	48.7%	42.2%
New York	9	James J. Delaney	D	49.7%	42.7%
New Jersey	4	Frank Thompson,Jr.	D	53.4%	46.4%
Montana	1	Arnold Olsen	D	53.6%	46.4%
Oklahoma	4	Tom Steed	D	53.6%	46.4%
North Carolina	6	L. Richardson Preyer	D	53.6%	46.4%
New York	34	James M. Hanley 1	D	51.3%	43.8%
California	15	John J. McFall	D	53.8%	46.2%
Iowa	4	John H. Kyl	R	53.9%	46.1%

State	CD	Incumbent	P	Incumbent	Challenger
Indiana	10	David W. Dennis	R	53.9%	46.1%
West Virginia	1	Robert H. Mollohan	D	53.9%	46.1%
Illinois	23	George E. Shipley	D	54.0%	46.0%
Illinois	3	William T. Murphy 1	D	54.0%	46.0%
North Carolina	3	David N. Henderson	D	54.0%	46.0%
Missouri	10	Bill D. Burlison	D	54.0%	46.0%
Illinois	21	Kenneth J. Gray	D	54.1%	45.9%
Alaska	AL	Howard W. Pollock 1	R	54.2%	45.8%
Virginia	2	G. William Whitehurst 2	R	54.2%	45.8%
Idaho	2	Orval H. Hansen 2	R	52.6%	43.9%
Indiana	9	Lee H. Hamilton	D	54.4%	45.6%
Connecticut	2	William L. St. Onge 1	D	54.1%	45.3%
New York	17	Edward I. Koch 2	D	51.7%	42.8%
Indiana	8	Roger H. Zion	R	54.5%	45.5%
Missouri	6	W.R.Hull 3	D	54.6%	45.4%
Ohio	22	Charles A. Vanik 2	D	54.7%	45.3%
Michigan	2	Marvin L. Esch	R	54.3%	44.9%
Colorado	4	Wayne N. Aspinall	D	54.7%	45.3%
North Carolina	10	James T. Broyhill	R	54.8%	45.2%
Florida	10	J. Herbert Burke	R	54.9%	45.1%
Oklahoma	2	Ed Edmondson	D	54.9%	45.1%
New Jersey	15	Edward J. Patten	D	54.6%	44.8%
Florida	7	James A. Haley	D	55.0%	45.0%
Indiana	2	Earl F. Landgrebe	R	55.1%	44.9%
Iowa	2	John C. Culver	D	55.1%	44.9%
Nebraska	2	Glenn Cunningham 1	R	55.2%	44.8%
Oklahoma	6	John N. Happy Camp 2	R	55.3%	44.7%
Nebraska	1	Robert V. Denney	R	54.1%	43.4%
Illinois	5	John C. Kluczynski	D	55.4%	44.6%
New Jersey	2	Charles W. Sandman, Jr.	R	55.3%	44.4%
Georgia	5	Fletcher Thompson	R	55.6%	44.4%
Virginia	7	John O. Marsh, Jr.	D	54.4%	43.2%
Maine	2	William D. Hathaway	D	55.7%	44.3%
Illinois	11	Roman C. Pucinski	D	55.8%	44.2%
Connecticut	3	Robert N. Giaimo	D	54.0%	42.4%
Texas	13	Graham Purcell	D	55.8%	44.2%
Kentucky	3	William O. Cowger	R	55.9%	44.1%
New York	3	Lester L. Wolff	D	52.1%	40.2%
Minnesota	6	John M. Zwach	R	56.2%	43.8%
Florida	9	Paul G. Rogers	D	56.2%	43.8%
Washington	2	Lloyd Meeds	D	56.2%	43.8%

State	CD	Incumbent	P	1968 Vote Incumbent	Challenger
Connecticut	5	John S. Monagan	D	56.3%	43.7%
New York	39	Richard D. McCarthy 1	D	54.6%	42.0%
Washington	6	Floyd V. Hicks	D	55.8%	43.1%
Kentucky	2	William H. Natcher	D	56.4%	43.6%
California	9	Don Edwards	D	56.6%	43.4%
Maine	1	Peter N. Kyros	D	56.6%	43.4%
Washington	5	Thomas S. Foley	D	56.8%	43.2%
Washington	3	Julia Butler Hansen	D	56.8%	43.2%
Indiana	1	Ray J. Madden	D	56.7%	43.0%
Pennsylvania	7	Lawrence G. Williams	R	56.5%	42.7%
Florida	12	Dante B. Fascell	D	57.0%	43.0%
Tennessee	3	W. E. Brock, III 1	R	57.0%	43.0%
California	4	Robert L. Leggett	D	55.6%	41.5%
Kentucky	6	John C. Watts	D	56.5%	42.4%
North Carolina	11	Roy A. TAYLOR	D	57.1%	42.9%
California	3	John E. Moss	D	56.0%	41.8%
Ohio	9	Thomas L. Ashley	D	57.4%	42.6%
New York	29	Daniel E. Button	R	56.9%	42.0%
Georgia	4	Ben Blackburn	R	57.5%	42.5%

DISTRICTS MADE MARGINAL BY THE RETIREMENT OF THE INCUMBENT

State	CD	Incumbent	P	1968 Vote Incumbent	Challenger
South Carolina	2	Albert W. Watson 1	R	57.6%	42.4%
South Dakota	1	Ben Reifel 1	R	58.0%	42.0%
Delaware	AL	William V. Roth, Jr. 1	R	58.7%	41.3%
South Dakota	2	E. Y. Berry 1	R	59.3%	40.7%
New York	25	Richard L. Ottinger 1,4	D	58.6%	34.7%
Connecticut	6	Thomas J. Meskill 1	R	62.3%	37.7%
Connecticut	1	Emilio Q. Daddario 1	D	62.4%	37.3%
Wyoming	AL	John S. Wold 1,2	R	62.7%	37.3%
Indiana	5	Richard L. Roudebush 1	R	63.0%	37.0%
California	38	John V. Tunney 1	D	62.7%	35.5%

B. ROLL CALL VOTES, 1968-1970

The Movement For a New Congress' scores[*] for members of the House and Senate from 1968 to 1970 are listed below. The scores equal the percentage of all roll calls on which each Congressman or Senator voted in accordance with the Movement's position (against the war and for domestic spending and civil rights). All roll calls dealing with these issues were included except those on which 80% or more of the membership voted on the same side of the question. Absences were not included in computing the scores.

The principal voting dimensions along which Democrats divide are sectional (North-South) and ideological (northern issue-oriented liberals versus northern old-line machine liberals), with Border State and Mountain State Democrats occupying the moderate, often pivotal position in Democratic voting.

Most House Republican liberals are from the Northeast. In the Senate the more liberal Republicans follow a similar geographic pattern but northeastern Senators are joined by several younger Senators from the Middle West and the Northwest who cast liberal votes on selected legislation.

The most important consideration in assessing such scores, however, is that they be viewed relatively. That is, a Democrat from North Carolina may have lower scores than his party brethren from New Jersey; yet his scores may be substantially higher than the rest of his state delegation. Therefore the simplest way of assessing these scores is by comparing the score of the member in whom you are interested with the scores of the other members from his state or immediate region. The data are arranged by region and by state in order to facilitate this comparison.

Keep in mind that roll calls represent only one stage, although an important one, of the legislative process. The public position taken by members on roll calls may not always be the same one that they have adopted in the crucial committee and pre-floor bargaining stages.

Note on the 1968 columns: Blanks indicate that the person was not yet a member of Congress in 1968. Zeros indicate zero scores for those who were members in 1968.

---

[*]These ratings are based on a study by William T. Murphy, Jr., at the Department of Politics, Princeton University.

NAME	P	STATE	D	DOM	DEP	TOT	DOM	DEP	TOT	DOM	DEP	TOT	DOM	DEP	TOT
DADDARIO	D	CONNECTICUT	1	94.1	75.0	90.5	100.0	75.0	87.5	83.3	75.0	81.3	91.9	75.0	86.8
GIAIMO	D	CONNECTICUT	3	70.6	75.0	71.4	25.0	18.2	21.1	50.0	50.0	50.0	53.8	35.3	48.2
WEICKER	R	CONNECTICUT	4				37.5	46.7	43.5	64.7	25.0	57.1	56.0	42.1	50.0
MONAGAN	D	CONNECTICUT	5	64.7	75.0	66.7	62.5	20.0	34.8	75.0	66.7	72.2	67.6	40.0	56.5
MESKILL	R	CONNECTICUT	6	60.0	0.0	47.4	25.0	15.4	19.0	46.2	25.0	41.2	47.2	14.3	35.1
KYROS	D	MAINE	1	94.1	75.0	90.5	83.3	40.0	52.4	87.5	60.0	81.0	89.7	50.0	74.6
HATHAWAY	D	MAINE	2	100.0	100.0	100.0	100.0	68.8	79.2	93.3	66.7	85.7	97.5	73.1	87.9
CONTE	R	MASSACHUSETTS	1	70.6	50.0	66.7	62.5	58.8	60.0	75.0	80.0	76.2	70.7	61.5	67.2
BOLAND	D	MASSACHUSETTS	2	92.9	75.0	88.9	75.0	58.8	64.0	76.5	50.0	69.6	82.1	59.3	72.7
PHILBIN	D	MASSACHUSETTS	3	94.1	66.7	90.0	62.5	17.6	32.0	82.4	20.0	68.2	83.3	24.0	61.2
DONOHUE	D	MASSACHUSETTS	4	100.0	75.0	95.0	62.5	31.3	41.7	82.4	50.0	73.9	85.4	42.3	68.7
MORSE	R	MASSACHUSETTS	5	76.5	50.0	73.7	87.5	76.5	80.0	71.4	100.0	80.0	76.9	80.0	78.1
HARRINGTON	D	MASSACHUSETTS	6				100.0	100.0	100.0	100.0	100.0	100.0	100.0	100.0	100.0
MACDONALD	D	MASSACHUSETTS	7	100.0	100.0	100.0	100.0	75.0	85.0	81.3	100.0	86.4	92.1	85.0	89.7
O'NEILL	D	MASSACHUSETTS	8	100.0	100.0	100.0	87.5	70.6	76.0	88.2	80.0	86.4	92.9	76.0	86.6
MCCORMACK	D	MASSACHUSETTS	9	SPEAKER OF THE HOUSE DOES NOT VOTE											
HECKLER	R	MASSACHUSETTS	10	87.5	50.0	80.0	50.0	64.7	60.0	84.6	83.3	84.2	78.4	66.7	73.4
BURKE, J.	D	MASSACHUSETTS	11	100.0	100.0	100.0	62.5	29.4	40.0	82.4	50.0	73.9	85.7	44.4	69.6
KEITH	R	MASSACHUSETTS	12	58.8	50.0	57.1	37.5	29.4	32.0	53.3	60.0	55.0	52.5	38.5	47.0
WYMAN	R	NEW HAMPSHIRE	1	29.4	50.0	33.3	12.5	6.7	8.7	17.6	0.0	13.0	21.4	12.0	17.9
CLEVELAND	R	NEW HAMPSHIRE	2	52.9	50.0	52.4	12.5	35.3	28.0	52.9	50.0	52.2	45.2	40.7	43.5
ST. GERMAIN	D	RHODE ISLAND	1	94.1	75.0	90.5	100.0	50.0	66.7	93.8	60.0	85.7	95.1	56.0	80.3
TIERNAN	D	RHODE ISLAND	2	94.1	75.0	90.5	87.5	56.3	66.7	87.5	66.7	81.8	90.2	61.5	79.1
STAFFORD	R	VERMONT	0	76.5	50.0	71.4	50.0	37.5	41.7	64.7	60.0	63.6	66.7	44.0	58.2

Name		State	No.												
ROTH	R	DELAWARE	0	40.0	50.0	42.1	16.7	23.5	21.7	41.2	16.7	34.8	36.8	25.9	32.3
HUNT	R	NEW JERSEY	1	23.5	50.0	28.6	12.5	6.7	8.7	17.6	0.0	13.0	19.0	12.0	16.4
SANDMAN	R	NEW JERSEY	2	29.4	50.0	33.3	25.0	0.0	10.5	29.4	16.7	26.1	28.6	14.3	23.8
HOWARD	D	NEW JERSEY	3	100.0	50.0	94.7	87.5	73.3	78.3	81.3	50.0	72.7	90.2	65.2	81.3
THOMPSON, F	D	NEW JERSEY	4	100.0	66.7	94.7	100.0	76.9	85.7	100.0	100.0	100.0	100.0	81.0	93.5
FRELINGHUYS	R	NEW JERSEY	5	62.5	100.0	68.4	50.0	25.0	33.3	56.3	16.7	45.5	57.5	32.0	47.7
WIDNALL	R	NEW JERSEY	7	73.3	50.0	68.4	37.5	13.3	21.7	41.2	20.0	36.4	52.5	20.8	40.6
ROE	D	NEW JERSEY	8	100.0	50.0		100.0	71.4	77.8	76.5	66.7	73.9	78.9	69.2	75.0
HELSTOSKI	D	NEW JERSEY	9	100.0	100.0	100.0	100.0	100.0	100.0	100.0	100.0	100.0	100.0	100.0	100.0
RODINO	D	NEW JERSEY	10	94.1	75.0	90.5	75.0	46.7	56.5	81.3	50.0	72.7	85.4	52.0	72.7
MINISH	D	NEW JERSEY	11	100.0	75.0	95.2	75.0	52.9	60.0	82.4	50.0	73.9	88.1	55.6	75.4
DWYER	R	NEW JERSEY	12	88.2	50.0	81.0	50.0	20.0	28.6	73.3	50.0	66.7	76.3	32.0	58.7
GALLAGHER	D	NEW JERSEY	13	100.0	100.0	100.0	100.0	30.0	56.3	100.0	60.0	90.0	100.0	52.6	82.4
DANIELS	D	NEW JERSEY	14	100.0	75.0	95.2	62.5	40.0	47.8	73.3	50.0	66.7	82.5	48.0	69.2
PATTEN	D	NEW JERSEY	15	94.1	75.0	90.5	75.0	47.1	56.0	81.3	66.7	77.3	85.4	55.6	73.5
PIKE	D	NEW YORK	1	70.6	50.0	66.7	62.5	75.0	70.8	70.6	100.0	77.3	69.0	76.0	71.6
GROVER	R	NEW YORK	2	47.1	25.0	42.9	12.5	13.3	13.0	26.7	0.0	19.0	32.5	12.0	24.6
WOLFF	D	NEW YORK	3	100.0	75.0	95.2	75.0	75.0	75.0	88.2	100.0	91.3	90.5	80.8	86.8
WYDLER	R	NEW YORK	4	70.6	50.0	66.7	37.5	35.7	36.4	56.3	66.7	59.1	58.5	45.8	53.8
LOWENSTEIN	D	NEW YORK	5	100.0	66.7		100.0	100.0	100.0	100.0	100.0	100.0	100.0	100.0	100.0
HALPERN	R	NEW YORK	6	100.0	66.7	95.0	83.3	69.2	73.7	81.3	100.0	85.7	89.7	76.2	85.0
ADDABBO	D	NEW YORK	7	94.1	75.0	90.5	62.5	58.8	60.0	100.0	66.7	90.9	90.2	63.0	79.4
ROSENTHAL	D	NEW YORK	8	100.0	100.0	100.0	100.0	100.0	100.0	100.0	100.0	100.0	100.0	100.0	100.0
DELANEY	D	NEW YORK	9	70.6	75.0	71.4	62.5	28.6	40.9	50.0	0.0	36.4	61.0	29.2	49.2
CELLER	D	NEW YORK	10	93.8	75.0	90.0	100.0	35.7	55.0	100.0	66.7	90.9	97.4	50.0	79.0

Name	Party	State	Dist	1	2	3	4	5	6	7	8	9	10	11	12
BRASCO	D	NEW YORK	11	100.0	75.0	95.2	100.0	100.0	100.0	100.0	100.0	100.0	100.0	96.0	98.5
CHISHOLM	D	NEW YORK	12				100.0	100.0	100.0	91.7	100.0	93.8	95.0	100.0	97.4
PODELL	D	NEW YORK	13	100.0	100.0	100.0	100.0	100.0	100.0	100.0	100.0	100.0	100.0	100.0	100.0
ROONEY, J.	D	NEW YORK	14	88.2	75.0	85.7	62.5	12.5	29.2	76.5	25.0	66.7	78.6	25.0	59.1
CAREY	D	NEW YORK	15	94.1	75.0	90.5	100.0	92.3	94.1	100.0	100.0	100.0	97.1	91.3	94.7
MURPHY, J.	D	NEW YORK	16	94.1	75.0	90.5	83.3	15.4	36.8	70.6	20.0	59.1	82.5	27.3	62.9
KOCH	D	NEW YORK	17				100.0	100.0	100.0	100.0	100.0	100.0	100.0	100.0	100.0
POWELL	D	NEW YORK	18				100.0	100.0	100.0	100.0	100.0	100.0	100.0	100.0	100.0
FARBSTEIN	D	NEW YORK	19	100.0	100.0	100.0	100.0	100.0	100.0	100.0	100.0	100.0	100.0	100.0	100.0
RYAN	D	NEW YORK	20	100.0	100.0	100.0	100.0	100.0	100.0	100.0	100.0	100.0	100.0	100.0	100.0
SCHEUER	D	NEW YORK	21	100.0	75.0	100.0	100.0	100.0	100.0	94.1	100.0	95.5	97.4	100.0	98.4
GILBERT	D	NEW YORK	22	100.0	75.0	95.0	100.0	94.1	96.0	100.0	100.0	100.0	100.0	92.3	96.9
BINGHAM	D	NEW YORK	23	100.0	100.0	100.0	100.0	100.0	100.0	88.2	100.0	91.3	95.2	100.0	97.0
BIAGGI	D	NEW YORK	24				62.5	41.2	48.0	68.8	20.0	57.1	66.7	36.4	52.2
OTTINGER	D	NEW YORK	25	87.5	75.0	85.0	100.0	100.0	100.0	100.0	100.0	100.0	94.1	96.0	94.9
REID, O.	R	NEW YORK	26	94.1	75.0	90.5	100.0	100.0	100.0	100.0	100.0	100.0	97.6	95.8	96.9
MCKNEALLY	R	NEW YORK	27				37.5	7.1	18.2	29.4	16.7	26.1	32.0	10.0	22.2
FISH	R	NEW YORK	28				66.7	31.3	40.9	43.8	40.0	42.9	50.0	33.3	41.9
BUTTON	R	NEW YORK	29	92.3	75.0	88.2	75.0	71.4	72.7	94.1	100.0	95.7	89.5	79.2	85.5
KING, C.J.	R	NEW YORK	30	20.0	0.0	15.8	12.5	6.3	8.3	11.8	0.0	8.7	15.0	3.8	10.6
MCEWEN	R	NEW YORK	31	21.4	50.0	27.8	12.5	17.6	16.0	14.3	20.0	15.8	16.7	23.1	19.4
PIRNIE	R	NEW YORK	32	52.9	50.0	52.4	60.0	6.7	20.0	41.2	16.7	34.8	48.7	16.0	35.9
ROBISON	R	NEW YORK	33	64.7	50.0	61.9	50.0	56.3	54.2	60.0	66.7	61.9	60.0	57.7	59.1
HANLEY	D	NEW YORK	34	82.4	75.0	81.0	62.5	43.8	50.0	76.5	60.0	72.7	76.2	52.0	67.2
STRATTON	D	NEW YORK	35	73.3	75.0	73.7	57.1	5.9	20.8	80.0	25.0	68.4	73.0	20.0	51.6

Name	Party	State	No.												
HORTON	R	NEW YORK	36	87.5	50.0	80.0	75.0	56.3	62.5	81.3	100.0	86.4	82.5	65.4	75.8
CONABLE	R	NEW YORK	37	60.0	50.0	58.3	25.0	30.8	28.6	47.1	16.7	39.1	45.7	28.6	39.3
HASTINGS	R	NEW YORK	38				0.0	10.0	7.1	30.8	16.7	26.3	23.5	12.5	18.2
MCCARTHY	D	NEW YORK	39	100.0	75.0	93.8	100.0	86.7	91.3	100.0	100.0	100.0	100.0	87.0	94.5
SMITH	R	NEW YORK	40				25.0	28.6	27.3	23.5	16.7	21.7	24.0	25.0	24.4
DULSKI	D	NEW YORK	41	100.0	75.0	95.0	62.5	37.5	45.8	82.4	66.7	78.3	85.4	50.0	71.6
BARRETT	D	PENNSYLVANIA	1	100.0	75.0	95.2	83.3	33.3	50.0	82.4	60.0	77.3	90.0	47.6	75.4
NIX	D	PENNSYLVANIA	2	100.0	75.0	95.2	100.0	60.0	73.9	88.2	100.0	90.9	95.2	70.8	86.4
BYRNE	D	PENNSYLVANIA	3	100.0	75.0	95.2	62.5	37.5	45.8	100.0	50.0	86.4	92.7	46.2	74.6
EILBERG	D	PENNSYLVANIA	4	85.7	75.0	83.3	87.5	40.0	61.1	100.0	66.7	91.3	92.3	55.0	79.7
GREEN, W.	D	PENNSYLVANIA	5	100.0	75.0	95.2	83.3	81.3	81.8	100.0	100.0	100.0	97.4	84.6	92.2
YATRON	D	PENNSYLVANIA	6				62.5	26.7	39.1	70.6	75.0	71.4	68.0	36.8	54.5
WILLIAMS, L	R	PENNSYLVANIA	7	25.0	50.0	30.0	12.5	11.8	12.0	11.8	16.7	13.0	17.1	18.5	17.6
BIESTER	R	PENNSYLVANIA	8	70.6	50.0	66.7	37.5	47.1	44.0	70.6	66.7	69.6	64.3	51.9	59.4
WATKINS	R	PENNSYLVANIA	9	21.4	25.0	22.2	20.0	7.1	10.5	28.6	0.0	21.1	24.2	8.7	17.9
MCDADE	R	PENNSYLVANIA	10	76.5	50.0	71.4	37.5	47.1	44.0	64.3	60.0	63.2	64.1	50.0	58.5
FLOOD	D	PENNSYLVANIA	11	62.5	66.7	63.2	62.5	20.0	34.8	56.3	33.3	50.0	60.0	29.2	48.4
WHALLEY	R	PENNSYLVANIA	12	11.8	50.0	19.0	20.0	11.1	14.3	29.4	0.0	22.7	20.5	16.7	19.3
COUGHLIN	R	PENNSYLVANIA	13				37.5	52.9	48.0	58.8	50.0	56.5	52.0	52.2	52.1
MOOREHEAD	D	PENNSYLVANIA	14	100.0	75.0	94.4	100.0	68.8	77.3	100.0	66.7	94.7	100.0	69.6	88.1
ROONEY, F.	D	PENNSYLVANIA	15	85.7	75.0	83.3	62.5	26.7	39.1	82.4	60.0	77.3	79.5	41.7	65.1
ESHLEMAN	R	PENNSYLVANIA	16	29.4	50.0	33.3	25.0	7.1	13.6	23.5	16.7	21.7	26.2	16.7	22.7
SCHNEEBELI	R	PENNSYLVANIA	17	23.5	75.0	33.3	12.5	40.0	30.4	30.8	66.7	37.5	23.7	50.0	33.3
CORBETT	R	PENNSYLVANIA	18	68.8	50.0	65.0	37.5	17.6	24.0	41.2	16.7	34.8	51.2	22.2	39.7
GOODLING	R	PENNSYLVANIA	19	11.8	25.0	14.3	0.0	15.4	10.0	12.5	20.0	14.3	10.0	18.2	12.9

Name	Party	State	No.												
GAYDOS	D	PENNSYLVANIA	20	93.8	75.0	90.0	62.5	56.3	58.3	84.6	75.0	82.4	76.2	60.0	68.3
DENT	D	PENNSYLVANIA	21	35.3	33.3	35.0	83.3	22.2	46.7	70.0	60.0	66.7	84.4	44.4	70.0
SAYLOR	R	PENNSYLVANIA	22	12.5	50.0	20.0	42.9	0.0	20.0	37.5	0.0	27.3	37.5	5.9	28.1
JOHNSON, A.	R	PENNSYLVANIA	23	70.6	75.0	71.4	25.0	0.0	10.0	14.3	16.7	15.0	15.8	13.6	15.0
VIGORITO	D	PENNSYLVANIA	24	75.0	100.0	78.9	62.5	43.8	50.0	70.6	60.0	68.2	69.0	52.0	62.7
CLARK	D	PENNSYLVANIA	25	94.1	75.0	90.5	62.5	7.7	28.6	57.1	20.0	47.4	65.8	23.8	50.8
MORGAN	D	PENNSYLVANIA	26	76.5	50.0	71.4	62.5	17.6	32.0	87.5	40.0	76.2	85.4	30.8	64.2
FULTON, J.	R	PENNSYLVANIA	27				62.5	17.6	32.0	73.3	66.7	71.4	72.5	33.3	56.7
DAWSON	D	ILLINOIS	1				100.0	0.0	75.0	75.0	0.0	75.0	90.0	0.0	75.0
MIKVA	D	ILLINOIS	2	100.0	75.0	100.0	100.0	100.0	100.0	100.0	100.0	100.0	100.0	100.0	100.0
MURPHY, W.	D	ILLINOIS	3	100.0	50.0	95.2	83.3	17.6	34.8	76.5	33.3	65.2	87.5	29.6	64.2
DERWINSKI	R	ILLINOIS	4	17.6	75.0	23.8	0.0	33.3	22.7	12.5	60.0	23.8	12.5	41.7	23.4
KLUCZYNSKI	D	ILLINOIS	5	94.1	75.0	90.5	60.0	18.8	28.6	76.9	16.7	57.9	82.9	26.9	59.0
ANNUNZIO	D	ILLINOIS	7	100.0	75.0	95.2	100.0	23.1	52.4	82.4	16.7	65.2	92.9	30.4	70.8
ROSTENKOWSK	D	ILLINOIS	8	88.2	100.0	85.7	62.5	18.2	36.8	68.8	16.7	54.5	75.6	28.6	59.7
YATES	D	ILLINOIS	9	88.2	0.0	90.5	100.0	88.2	92.0	100.0	100.0	100.0	94.9	92.6	93.9
COLLIER	R	ILLINOIS	10	11.8	75.0	9.5	0.0	6.7	4.3	23.5	0.0	17.4	14.3	4.0	10.4
PUCINSKI	D	ILLINOIS	11	62.5	50.0	65.0	62.5	30.8	42.9	52.9	16.7	43.5	58.5	34.8	50.0
MCCLORY	R	ILLINOIS	12	38.5		41.2	37.5	11.8	20.0	47.1	16.7	39.1	42.1	18.5	32.3
CRANE	R	ILLINOIS	13				0.0	16.7	12.5	11.8	0.0	9.5	10.5	10.0	10.3
ERLENBORN	R	ILLINOIS	14	35.3	50.0	38.1	0.0	20.0	13.0	27.3	16.7	23.5	25.0	24.0	24.6
REID, C.	R	ILLINOIS	15	11.8	0.0	9.5	0.0	6.3	4.5	40.0	0.0	28.6	21.1	3.8	14.1
ANDERSON, J	R	ILLINOIS	16	52.9	50.0	52.4	25.0	20.0	21.7	35.3	0.0	28.6	40.5	21.7	33.8
ARENDS	R	ILLINOIS	17	6.7	66.7	16.7	0.0	6.7	4.3	23.5	16.7	21.7	12.5	16.7	14.1
MICHEL	R	ILLINOIS	18	41.2	25.0	38.1	0.0	13.3	8.7	18.8	0.0	14.3	24.4	12.5	20.0

Name	Party	State	No.											
RAILSBACK	R	ILLINOIS	19	70.6	50.0	66.7	50.0	27.3	36.8	57.1	50.0	55.6	61.5	36.8	53.4
FINDLEY	R	ILLINOIS	20	41.2	0.0	33.3	25.0	42.9	36.4	46.7	16.7	38.1	40.0	29.2	35.9
GRAY	D	ILLINOIS	21	85.7	75.0	83.3	62.5	17.6	32.0	75.0	16.7	59.1	76.3	25.9	55.4
SPRINGER	R	ILLINOIS	22	41.2	50.0	42.9	25.0	7.7	14.3	37.5	16.7	31.8	36.6	17.4	29.7
SHIPLEY	D	ILLINOIS	23	70.6	75.0	71.4	50.0	25.0	31.8	50.0	66.7	54.5	59.0	42.3	52.3
PRICE, M.	D	ILLINOIS	24	100.0	75.0	94.7	62.5	17.6	32.0	76.5	25.0	66.7	82.5	28.0	61.5
MADDEN	D	INDIANA	1	100.0	75.0	95.2	87.5	50.0	62.5	81.3	50.0	75.0	90.2	54.2	76.9
LANDGREBE	R	INDIANA	2				0.0	6.7	4.5	17.6	16.7	17.4	12.5	9.5	11.1
BRADEMAS	D	INDIANA	3	100.0	75.0	94.4	87.5	69.2	76.2	87.5	83.3	86.4	92.1	73.9	85.2
ADAIR	R	INDIANA	4	16.7	50.0	25.0	25.0	6.7	13.0	20.0	16.7	19.0	20.0	16.0	18.3
ROUDEBUSH	R	INDIANA	5	8.3	50.0	18.8	0.0	6.3	4.2	16.7	50.0	21.4	9.4	18.2	13.0
BRAY	R	INDIANA	6	17.6	33.3	20.0	0.0	11.8	8.0	11.8	20.0	13.6	11.9	16.0	13.4
MYERS	R	INDIANA	7	17.6	50.0	23.8	0.0	11.8	8.0	28.6	16.7	25.0	17.9	18.5	18.2
ZION	R	INDIANA	8	14.3	0.0	11.1	12.5	6.3	8.3	17.6	16.7	17.4	15.4	7.7	12.3
HAMILTON	D	INDIANA	9	76.5	75.0	76.2	62.5	47.1	52.0	76.9	50.0	68.4	73.7	51.9	64.6
DENNIS	R	INDIANA	10				0.0	17.6	12.0	29.4	16.7	26.1	20.0	17.8	18.8
JACOBS	D	INDIANA	11	100.0	75.0	94.1	75.0	56.3	62.5	81.3	80.0	81.0	86.5	64.0	77.4
CONYERS	D	MICHIGAN	1	100.0	100.0	100.0	100.0	100.0	100.0	100.0	100.0	100.0	100.0	100.0	100.0
ESCH	R	MICHIGAN	2	76.5	50.0	71.4	60.0	42.9	47.4	77.8	80.0	78.6	74.2	52.2	64.8
BROWN, G.E.	R	MICHIGAN	3	58.8	25.0	52.4	42.9	43.8	43.5	33.3	20.0	30.0	46.2	36.0	42.2
HUTCHINSON	R	MICHIGAN	4	29.4	50.0	33.3	0.0	18.8	12.5	17.6	16.7	17.4	19.0	23.1	20.6
FORD, G.	R	MICHIGAN	5	43.8	66.7	47.4	0.0	11.8	8.3	23.5	20.0	22.7	27.5	20.0	24.6
CHAMBERLAIN	R	MICHIGAN	6	41.2	50.0	42.9	25.0	11.8	16.0	28.6	16.7	25.0	33.3	18.5	27.3
RIEGLE	R	MICHIGAN	7	70.6	50.0	66.7	50.0	61.5	57.1	57.1	100.0	66.7	61.5	66.7	63.3
HARVEY	R	MICHIGAN	8	64.7	50.0	61.9	50.0	28.6	35.0	29.4	16.7	26.1	47.5	29.2	40.6

Name	Party	State	No.												
VANDER JAGT	R	MICHIGAN	9	58.8	50.0	57.1	37.5	37.5	37.5	46.7	100.0	60.0	50.0	52.0	50.8
CEDERBERG	R	MICHIGAN	10	38.5	33.3	37.5	16.7	6.7	9.5	14.3	16.7	15.0	24.2	12.5	19.3
RUPPE	R	MICHIGAN	11	81.3	50.0	75.0	71.4	40.0	50.0	35.7	50.0	40.0	62.2	44.0	54.8
O'HARA, J.	D	MICHIGAN	12	100.0	100.0	100.0	87.5	58.8	68.0	100.0	83.3	95.2	97.4	69.2	86.2
DIGGS	D	MICHIGAN	13	100.0	100.0	100.0	100.0	93.3	95.7	92.9	100.0	94.4	97.4	95.5	96.7
NEDZI	D	MICHIGAN	14	88.2	75.0	85.7	87.5	76.5	80.0	94.1	100.0	95.7	90.5	81.5	87.0
FORD, W.	D	MICHIGAN	15	100.0	75.0	95.0	75.0	68.8	70.8	100.0	83.3	95.5	95.0	73.1	86.4
DINGELL	D	MICHIGAN	16	87.5	100.0	89.5	75.0	58.3	65.0	92.9	25.0	77.8	86.8	57.9	77.2
GRIFFITHS	D	MICHIGAN	17	100.0	100.0	100.0	71.4	54.5	61.1	84.6	66.7	78.9	87.9	65.0	79.2
BROOMFIELD	R	MICHIGAN	18	64.7	50.0	61.9	28.6	11.8	16.7	50.0	40.0	47.6	52.5	23.1	40.9
MCDONALD	R	MICHIGAN	19	52.9	50.0	52.4	37.5	35.3	36.0	46.2	20.0	38.9	47.4	34.6	42.2
TAFT	R	OHIO	1	80.0	50.0	73.7	33.3	15.4	21.1	33.3	0.0	26.7	54.5	20.0	41.5
CLANCY	R	OHIO	2	11.8	0.0	9.5	0.0	7.1	4.5	13.3	0.0	9.5	10.0	4.2	7.8
WHALEN	R	OHIO	3	88.2	50.0	81.0	100.0	73.3	82.6	76.5	100.0	82.6	85.7	76.0	82.1
MCCULLOCH	R	OHIO	4	62.5	50.0	60.0	50.0	8.3	25.0	41.2	0.0	30.4	51.2	13.6	38.1
LATTA	R	OHIO	5	23.5	50.0	28.6	12.5	12.5	12.5	29.4	16.7	26.1	23.8	19.2	22.1
HARSHA	R	OHIO	6	14.3	33.3	17.6	12.5	6.3	8.3	29.4	0.0	21.7	20.5	8.0	15.6
BROWN, C.	R	OHIO	7	41.2	50.0	42.9	37.5	13.3	21.7	41.2	20.0	36.4	40.5	20.8	33.3
BETTS	R	OHIO	8	23.5	50.0	28.6	0.0	15.4	9.5	18.8	16.7	18.2	17.1	21.7	18.8
ASHLEY	D	OHIO	9	93.8	66.7	89.5	100.0	66.7	78.3	82.4	100.0	87.0	90.2	75.0	84.6
MILLER, C.	R	OHIO	10	11.8	50.0	19.0	12.5	11.8	12.0	29.4	66.7	39.1	19.0	29.6	23.2
STANTON	R	OHIO	11	76.5	33.3	70.0	37.5	18.8	25.0	56.3	50.0	54.5	61.0	28.0	48.5
DEVINE	R	OHIO	12	11.8	0.0	9.5	0.0	7.1	4.5	11.8	0.0	8.7	9.5	4.2	7.6
MOSHER	R	OHIO	13	81.3	50.0	75.0	50.0	69.2	61.9	70.6	100.0	78.3	70.7	73.9	71.9
AYRES	R	OHIO	14	56.3	50.0	55.0	12.5	7.1	9.1	54.5	25.0	46.7	45.7	18.2	35.1

Name	Party	State	No.												
WYLIE	R	OHIO	15	35.3	50.0	38.1	25.0	7.1	13.6	26.7	0.0	19.0	30.0	12.5	23.4
BOW	R	OHIO	16	31.3	25.0	30.0	16.7	0.0	5.9	28.6	0.0	20.0	27.8	4.8	19.3
ASHBROOK	R	OHIO	17	6.7	0.0	5.6	0.0	25.0	15.0	23.5	0.0	19.0	12.5	15.8	13.6
HAYS	D	OHIO	18	63.6	66.7	64.3	62.5	10.0	33.3	53.3	20.0	45.0	58.8	22.2	46.2
KIRWAN	D	OHIO	19	71.4	75.0	72.2	75.0	0.0	75.0	75.0	0.0	60.0	72.7	60.0	70.4
FEIGHAN	D	OHIO	20	88.2	75.0	85.7	62.5	23.5	36.0	71.4	60.0	68.4	76.9	38.5	61.5
STOKES	D	OHIO	21				100.0	94.1	96.0	94.1	100.0	95.7	96.0	95.7	95.8
VANIK	D	OHIO	22	81.3	75.0	80.0	75.0	64.7	68.0	94.1	100.0	95.7	85.4	74.1	80.9
MINSHALL	R	OHIO	23	61.5	0.0	47.1	33.3	12.5	15.8	50.0	16.7	40.0	53.3	11.5	33.9
LUKENS	R	OHIO	24	17.6	33.3	20.0	50.0	11.8	21.7	14.3	0.0	10.0	23.3	13.0	18.9
SCHADEBERG	R	WISCONSIN	1	23.5	0.0	19.0	0.0	5.9	4.0	29.4	0.0	22.7	21.4	3.8	14.7
KASTENMEIER	D	WISCONSIN	2	100.0	75.0	95.2	100.0	100.0	100.0	100.0	100.0	100.0	100.0	96.3	98.6
THOMSON	R	WISCONSIN	3	23.5	25.0	23.8	12.5	12.5	12.5	17.6	16.7	17.4	19.0	15.4	17.6
ZABLOCKI	D	WISCONSIN	4	85.7	75.0	83.3	62.5	17.6	32.0	58.8	16.7	47.8	69.2	25.9	51.5
REUSS	D	WISCONSIN	5	94.1	75.0	90.5	100.0	76.5	84.0	100.0	100.0	100.0	97.6	80.8	91.0
STEIGER, W.	R	WISCONSIN	6	64.7	50.0	61.9	50.0	18.8	29.2	25.0	0.0	20.0	46.3	20.8	36.9
OBEY	D	WISCONSIN	7				83.3	64.7	69.6	81.3	60.0	76.2	81.8	63.6	72.7
BYRNES	R	WISCONSIN	8	29.4	50.0	31.6	0.0	12.5	8.3	23.5	16.7	21.7	21.4	16.7	19.7
DAVIS	R	WISCONSIN	9				0.0	14.3	9.1	11.8	0.0	8.7	8.0	10.0	8.9
O'KONSKI	R	WISCONSIN	10	61.5	0.0	47.1	37.5	20.0	26.1	62.5	60.0	61.9	56.8	25.0	44.3
SCHWENGEL	R	IOWA	1	57.1	50.0	55.6	50.0	40.0	43.5	43.8	40.0	42.9	50.0	41.7	46.8
CULVER	D	IOWA	2	87.5	75.0	85.0	100.0	64.7	73.9	100.0	100.0	100.0	94.6	73.1	85.7
GROSS	R	IOWA	3	11.8	0.0	9.5	0.0	35.3	24.0	23.5	0.0	17.4	14.3	22.2	17.4
KYL	R	IOWA	4	17.6	33.3	20.0	12.5	6.7	8.7	41.2	16.7	34.8	26.2	12.5	21.2
SMITH, N.	D	IOWA	5	52.9	75.0	57.1	50.0	35.7	40.9	46.7	16.7	38.1	50.0	37.5	45.3

Name	Party	State	District												
MAYNE	R	IOWA	6	14.3	50.0	22.2	0.0	23.5	16.0	31.3	20.0	28.6	18.4	26.9	21.9
SCHERLE	R	IOWA	7	17.6	0.0	15.0	0.0	6.3	4.2	20.0	0.0	14.3	15.0	4.0	10.8
SEBELIUS	R	KANSAS	1				0.0	7.7	5.0	13.3	0.0	9.5	9.1	5.3	7.3
MIZE	R	KANSAS	2	37.5	33.3	36.8	25.0	6.7	13.0	25.0	16.7	22.7	30.0	12.5	23.4
WINN	R	KANSAS	3	29.4	50.0	33.3	14.3	8.3	10.5	11.8	16.7	13.0	19.5	18.2	19.0
SHRIVER	R	KANSAS	4	35.3	50.0	38.1	37.5	6.3	16.7	12.5	16.7	13.6	26.8	15.4	22.4
SKUBITZ	R	KANSAS	5	23.5	50.0	28.6	37.5	18.8	25.0	25.0	16.7	22.7	26.8	23.1	25.4
QUIE	R	MINNESOTA	1	64.7	50.0	61.9	12.5	28.6	22.7	47.1	16.7	39.1	47.6	29.2	40.9
NELSEN	R	MINNESOTA	2	37.5	33.3	36.8	12.5	6.3	8.3	29.4	16.7	26.1	29.3	12.0	22.7
MACGREGOR	R	MINNESOTA	3	56.3	33.3	52.6	42.9	20.0	27.3	35.7	20.0	31.6	45.9	21.7	36.7
KARTH	D	MINNESOTA	4	84.6	75.0	82.4	87.5	58.8	68.0	93.8	100.0	95.5	89.2	70.4	81.3
FRASER	D	MINNESOTA	5	94.1	100.0	95.0	100.0	94.1	96.0	100.0	100.0	100.0	97.6	96.2	97.0
ZWACH	R	MINNESOTA	6	47.1	50.0	47.6	25.0	21.4	22.7	53.3	0.0	38.1	45.0	20.8	35.9
LANGEN	R	MINNESOTA	7	17.6	0.0	14.3	12.5	6.3	8.3	29.4	0.0	25.0	21.4	4.3	15.4
BLATNIK	D	MINNESOTA	8	88.2	75.0	85.7	100.0	50.0	64.7	85.7	50.0	75.0	88.9	54.5	75.9
CLAY	D	MISSOURI	1				100.0	100.0	100.0	93.8	100.0	95.0	95.8	100.0	97.8
SYMINGTON	D	MISSOURI	2				75.0	47.1	56.0	75.0	60.0	71.4	75.0	50.0	63.0
SULLIVAN	D	MISSOURI	3	86.7	75.0	84.2	83.3	41.7	55.6	64.7	40.0	59.1	76.3	47.6	66.1
RANDALL	D	MISSOURI	4	35.3	50.0	38.1	37.5	17.6	24.0	29.4	16.7	26.1	33.3	22.2	29.0
BOLLING	D	MISSOURI	5	93.8	75.0	90.0	100.0	54.5	73.7	100.0	80.0	94.1	97.2	65.0	85.7
HULL	D	MISSOURI	6	14.3	25.0	16.7	12.5	9.1	10.5	29.4	0.0	21.7	20.5	9.5	16.7
HALL	R	MISSOURI	7	11.8	0.0	9.5	0.0	5.9	4.0	26.7	0.0	19.0	15.0	3.7	10.4
ICHORD	D	MISSOURI	8	21.4	50.0	27.8	12.5	5.9	8.0	31.3	16.7	27.3	23.7	14.8	20.0
HUNGATE	D	MISSOURI	9	53.8	75.0	58.8	62.5	52.9	56.0	43.8	40.0	42.9	51.4	53.8	52.4
BURLISON	D	MISSOURI	10				62.5	50.0	54.2	47.1	50.0	47.8	52.0	50.0	51.1

Name		State	Dist												
DENNEY	R	NEBRASKA	1	11.8	50.0	19.0	0.0	8.3	5.0	17.6	20.0	18.2	11.9	19.0	14.3
CUNNINGHAM	R	NEBRASKA	2	46.2	33.3	43.8	28.6	7.7	15.0	26.7	40.0	30.0	34.3	19.0	28.6
MARTIN	R	NEBRASKA	3	14.3	25.0	16.7	0.0	15.4	9.5	25.0	0.0	19.0	15.8	13.6	15.0
ANDREWS, M.	R	NORTH DAKOTA	1	52.9	50.0	52.4	37.5	13.3	21.7	31.3	16.7	27.3	41.5	20.0	33.3
KLEPPE	R	NORTH DAKOTA	2	35.3	50.0	38.1	12.5	12.5	12.5	21.4	16.7	20.0	25.6	19.2	23.1
REIFEL	R	SOUTH DAKOTA	1	52.9	33.3	50.0	25.0	0.0	11.1	30.8	20.0	27.8	39.5	11.1	30.4
BERRY	R	SOUTH DAKOTA	2	13.3	33.3	16.7	0.0	9.1	5.9	21.4	25.0	22.2	14.3	16.7	15.1
EDWARDS, J.	R	ALABAMA	1	18.8	0.0	15.8	0.0	6.7	4.8	5.9	0.0	4.8	10.3	4.5	8.2
DICKINSON	R	ALABAMA	2	6.7	0.0	5.3	0.0	0.0	0.0	6.3	0.0	4.5	5.3	0.0	3.3
ANDREWS, G.	D	ALABAMA	3	12.5	0.0	10.0	0.0	6.3	4.2	31.3	0.0	23.8	17.5	4.0	12.3
NICHOLS	D	ALABAMA	4	7.7	0.0	6.3	12.5	8.3	10.0	26.7	0.0	20.0	16.7	5.0	12.5
FLOWERS	D	ALABAMA	5				12.5	16.7	15.0	12.5	0.0	10.0	12.5	12.5	12.5
BUCHANAN	R	ALABAMA	6	17.6	0.0	14.3	0.0	7.1	4.5	11.8	20.0	13.6	11.9	8.7	10.8
BEVILL	D	ALABAMA	7	20.0	0.0	16.7	12.5	5.9	8.0	29.4	20.0	27.3	22.5	8.0	16.9
JONES, R.	D	ALABAMA	8	47.1	66.7	50.0	80.0	18.8	33.3	46.2	16.7	36.8	51.4	24.0	40.0
ALEXANDER	D	ARKANSAS	1				83.3	13.3	33.3	20.0	20.0	20.0	38.1	15.0	26.8
MILLS	D	ARKANSAS	2	12.5	0.0	10.0	50.0	14.3	33.3	33.3	0.0	25.0	28.2	6.3	21.8
HAMMERSCHMIDT	R	ARKANSAS	3	12.5	50.0	20.0	33.3	12.5	18.2	17.6	16.7	17.4	17.9	19.2	18.5
PRYOR	D	ARKANSAS	4				62.5	33.3	43.5	50.0	50.0	50.0	54.2	38.1	46.7
SIKES	D	FLORIDA	1	43.8	0.0	35.0	0.0	6.3	4.2	17.6	0.0	13.6	24.4	4.0	16.7
FUQUA	D	FLORIDA	2	29.4	0.0	23.8	0.0	6.3	4.5	17.6	0.0	13.6	20.0	4.0	13.8
BENNETT	D	FLORIDA	3	11.8	75.0	23.8	0.0	11.8	8.0	35.3	16.7	30.4	19.0	22.2	20.3
CHAPPELL	D	FLORIDA	4				0.0	6.7	4.3	23.5	0.0	17.4	16.0	4.8	10.9
FREY	R	FLORIDA	5				0.0	7.7	4.8	7.1	0.0	5.3	4.5	5.6	5.0
GIBBONS	D	FLORIDA	6	43.8	50.0	44.4	62.5	20.0	38.9	53.3	60.0	55.0	51.3	35.3	46.4

Name	Party	State	Dist.												
HALEY	D	FLORIDA	7	17.6	0.0	14.3	0.0	6.7	4.3	25.0	0.0	18.2	17.1	4.0	12.1
CRAMER	R	FLORIDA	8	11.8	0.0	9.5	0.0	7.1	4.5	7.7	33.3	15.8	7.9	12.5	9.7
ROGERS, P.	D	FLORIDA	9	12.5	0.0	10.0	0.0	11.8	8.0	35.3	16.7	30.4	19.5	11.1	16.2
BURKE, J.H.	R	FLORIDA	10	6.7	0.0	5.3	0.0	12.5	8.3	13.3	0.0	9.5	7.9	7.7	7.8
PEPPER	D	FLORIDA	11	87.5	66.7	84.2	71.4	33.3	50.0	66.7	40.0	60.0	76.3	41.2	65.5
FASCELL	D	FLORIDA	12	69.2	75.0	70.6	57.1	22.2	37.5	66.7	75.0	68.4	65.7	47.1	59.6
HAGAN	D	GEORGIA	1	20.0	0.0	15.8	0.0	6.3	4.2	25.0	0.0	19.0	17.9	4.0	12.5
O'NEAL	D	GEORGIA	2	11.8	0.0	9.5	0.0	0.0	0.0	20.0	0.0	14.3	12.5	0.0	8.3
BRINKLEY	D	GEORGIA	3	23.5	0.0	19.0	12.5	5.9	8.0	17.6	0.0	13.0	19.0	3.7	13.0
BLACKBURN	R	GEORGIA	4	13.3	0.0	10.5	0.0	13.3	8.7	6.3	0.0	4.5	7.7	8.0	7.8
THOMPSON	R	GEORGIA	5	23.5	0.0	19.0	12.5	5.9	8.0	5.9	0.0	4.3	14.3	3.7	10.1
FLYNT	D	GEORGIA	6	17.6	0.0	14.3	0.0	8.3	5.6	29.4	0.0	21.7	20.0	4.5	14.5
DAVIS, J.	D	GEORGIA	7	33.3	50.0	36.8	12.5	7.7	9.5	21.4	0.0	15.0	24.3	13.0	20.0
STUCKEY	D	GEORGIA	8	18.8	0.0	15.0	12.5	0.0	5.0	23.5	0.0	18.2	19.5	0.0	12.9
LANDRUM	D	GEORGIA	9	16.7	33.3	20.0	16.7	8.3	11.1	25.0	0.0	20.0	20.6	10.5	17.0
STEPHENS	D	GEORGIA	10	41.2	50.0	42.9	25.0	10.0	16.7	18.8	0.0	13.6	29.3	15.0	24.6
HEBERT	D	LOUISIANA	1	26.7	66.7	33.3	0.0	0.0	0.0	23.5	16.7	21.7	20.0	12.5	17.2
BOGGS	D	LOUISIANA	2	82.4	66.7	80.0	57.1	14.3	28.6	76.5	16.7	60.9	75.6	21.7	56.3
CAFFERY	D	LOUISIANA	3				0.0	12.5	8.3	25.0	0.0	18.2	16.7	9.1	13.0
WAGGONNER	D	LOUISIANA	4	35.7	0.0	27.8	0.0	5.9	4.0	17.6	0.0	13.0	20.5	3.7	13.6
PASSMAN	D	LOUISIANA	5	17.6	0.0	15.0	0.0	6.3	4.2	12.5	0.0	10.0	12.2	4.3	9.4
RARICK	D	LOUISIANA	6	0.0	0.0	0.0	0.0	20.0	14.3	11.8	0.0	8.7	5.6	12.0	8.2
EDWARDS	D	LOUISIANA	7	36.4	75.0	46.7	50.0	8.3	22.2	35.7	0.0	26.3	38.7	19.0	30.8
LONG, S.	D	LOUISIANA	8	9.1	25.0	13.3	0.0	7.1	4.5	18.8	0.0	13.6	11.4	8.3	10.2
ABERNATHY	D	MISSISSIPPI	1	5.9	0.0	5.0	0.0	6.7	4.3	17.6	0.0	13.6	9.5	4.3	7.7

Representative	Party	State	Dist											
WHITTEN	D	MISSISSIPPI	2	12.5	10.0	0.0	7.7	4.8	17.6	0.0	13.6	12.2	4.5	9.5
GRIFFIN	D	MISSISSIPPI	3	23.5	22.2	0.0	0.0	0.0	17.6	0.0	13.0	16.7	0.0	12.1
MONTGOMERY	D	MISSISSIPPI	4	5.9	4.8	0.0	6.3	4.2	13.3	0.0	9.5	7.5	3.8	6.1
COLMER	D	MISSISSIPPI	5	6.3	10.0	0.0	9.1	5.9	12.5	0.0	9.1	7.9	9.5	8.5
JONES, W.	D	NORTH CAROLINA	1	23.5	23.8	12.5	6.7	8.7	31.3	0.0	22.7	24.4	8.0	18.2
FOUNTAIN	D	NORTH CAROLINA	2	17.6	23.8	0.0	6.3	4.2	11.8	20.0	13.6	11.9	16.0	13.4
HENDERSON	D	NORTH CAROLINA	3	17.6	19.0	12.5	7.1	9.1	26.7	0.0	20.0	20.0	8.7	15.9
GALIFIANAKI	D	NORTH CAROLINA	4	40.0	42.1	25.0	21.4	22.7	52.9	33.3	47.8	42.5	29.2	37.5
MIZELL	R	NORTH CAROLINA	5			0.0	6.7	4.3	5.9	0.0	4.3	4.0	4.8	4.3
PREYER	D	NORTH CAROLINA	6		50.0	50.0	23.1	33.3	52.9	40.0	50.0	52.0	27.8	41.9
LENNON	D	NORTH CAROLINA	7	17.6		0.0	6.3	4.2	35.7	0.0	25.0	20.5	3.8	13.8
RUTH	R	NORTH CAROLINA	8		14.3	0.0	5.9	4.0	18.8	20.0	19.0	12.5	9.1	10.9
JONAS	R	NORTH CAROLINA	9	11.8	19.0	0.0	11.8	8.0	5.9	16.7	8.7	7.1	18.5	11.6
BROYHILL, J R	R	NORTH CAROLINA	10	11.8	9.5	0.0	18.8	12.5	11.8	0.0	8.7	9.5	11.5	10.3
TAYLOR	D	NORTH CAROLINA	11	29.4	33.3	25.0	6.7	13.0	47.1	0.0	34.8	35.7	12.0	26.9
RIVERS	D	SOUTH CAROLINA	1	23.5	20.0	0.0	0.0	0.0	15.4	0.0	11.1	16.7	0.0	10.9
WATSON	R	SOUTH CAROLINA	2	17.6	14.3	0.0	6.3	4.2	7.7	0.0	5.6	10.5	4.0	7.9
DORN	D	SOUTH CAROLINA	3	17.6	15.0	37.5	6.7	17.4	31.3	0.0	23.8	26.8	4.3	18.8
MANN	D	SOUTH CAROLINA	4			25.0	7.1	13.6	15.4	0.0	11.8	19.0	5.6	12.8
GETTYS	D	SOUTH CAROLINA	5	20.0	26.3	14.3	0.0	7.1	14.3	0.0	10.5	16.7	12.5	15.4
MCMILLAN	D	SOUTH CAROLINA	6	18.8	15.0	0.0	7.7	4.8	15.4	0.0	13.3	13.5	5.3	10.7
PATMAN	D	TEXAS	1	75.0	75.0	83.3	0.0	33.3	28.6	20.0	26.3	58.3	22.2	46.3
DOWDY	D	TEXAS	2	18.8	16.7	0.0	6.3	4.2	11.8	0.0	8.7	12.2	4.2	9.2
COLLINS	D	TEXAS	3	25.0	25.0	0.0	20.0	13.0	5.9	0.0	4.3	6.9	14.3	10.0
ROBERTS	D	TEXAS	4	17.6	14.3	12.5	7.7	9.5	31.3	0.0	22.7	22.0	4.3	15.6

CABELL	D	TEXAS	5	17.6	0.0	14.3	12.5	0.0	0.0	5.9	38.5	0.0	27.8	23.7	0.0	16.1
TEAGUE, O.	D	TEXAS	6	16.7	0.0	12.5	0.0	0.0	0.0	0.0	15.4	16.7	15.8	12.1	5.3	9.6
BUSH	R	TEXAS	7	29.4	50.0	33.3	0.0	25.0	15.0	15.0	27.3	0.0	23.1	22.2	27.8	24.1
ECKHARDT	D	TEXAS	8	94.1	75.0	90.5	100.0	100.0	76.9	85.7	100.0	100.0	100.0	97.6	82.6	92.2
BROOKS	D	TEXAS	9	64.7	75.0	66.7	83.3		37.5	57.1	40.0	0.0	30.0	57.9	35.3	50.9
PICKLE	D	TEXAS	10	45.5	75.0	53.3	50.0		15.4	28.6	35.3	16.7	30.4	41.7	26.1	35.6
POAGE	D	TEXAS	11	21.4	50.0	27.8	25.0		8.3	15.0	31.3	0.0	26.3	26.3	15.8	22.8
WRIGHT	D	TEXAS	12	52.9	75.0	57.1	83.3		20.0	38.1	47.1	16.7	39.1	55.0	28.0	44.6
PURCELL	D	TEXAS	13	20.0	25.0	21.1	40.0		23.1	27.8	14.3	25.0	16.7	20.6	23.8	21.8
YOUNG	D	TEXAS	14	64.7	100.0	70.0	62.5		11.1	35.3	41.2	16.7	34.8	54.8	27.8	46.7
DE LA GARZA	D	TEXAS	15	52.9	50.0	52.6	50.0		28.6	36.4	64.3	16.7	50.0	56.4	27.3	45.9
WHITE	D	TEXAS	16	35.3	50.0	38.1	62.5		12.5	29.2	50.0	16.7	40.9	46.3	19.2	35.8
BURLESON	D	TEXAS	17	11.8	0.0	9.5	0.0		5.9	4.0	23.5	0.0	17.4	14.3	3.7	10.1
PRICE, R.	R	TEXAS	18	11.8	0.0	9.5	0.0		6.7	4.3	0.0	0.0	0.0	4.9	4.0	4.5
MAHON	D	TEXAS	19	23.5	50.0	28.6	0.0		5.9	4.3	25.0	16.7	22.7	20.5	14.8	18.2
GONZALEZ	D	TEXAS	20	94.1	75.0	90.5	62.5		29.4	40.0	70.6	33.3	60.9	78.6	37.0	62.3
FISHER	D	TEXAS	21	23.5	0.0	19.0	12.5		6.7	8.7	17.6	0.0	14.3	19.0	4.3	13.8
CASEY	D	TEXAS	22	29.4	0.0	23.8	25.0		7.1	13.6	29.4	0.0	21.7	28.6	4.2	19.7
KAZEN	D	TEXAS	23	64.7	75.0	66.7	50.0		23.5	32.0	47.1	16.7	39.1	54.8	29.6	44.9
DOWNING	D	VIRGINIA	1	29.4	25.0	28.6	25.0		6.3	12.5	29.4	0.0	22.7	28.6	8.0	20.9
WHITEHURST	R	VIRGINIA	2				37.5		6.3	16.7	56.3	0.0	42.9	50.0	4.8	28.9
SATTERFIELD	D	VIRGINIA	3	11.8	0.0	9.5	0.0		5.9	4.0	17.6	0.0	13.6	11.9	3.8	8.8
ABBITT	D	VIRGINIA	4	12.5	0.0	10.0	0.0		10.0	6.3	12.5	0.0	9.1	10.5	5.0	8.6
DANIEL	D	VIRGINIA	5				0.0		6.3	4.2	17.6	0.0	13.6	12.0	4.8	8.7
POFF	R	VIRGINIA	6	11.8	50.0	19.0	0.0		11.8	8.0	11.8	16.7	13.0	9.5	18.5	13.0

Name	Party	State	Dist.												
MARSH	D	VIRGINIA	7	17.6	0.0	14.3	0.0	11.8	8.0	11.8	0.0	8.7	11.9	7.4	10.1
SCOTT	R	VIRGINIA	8	7.7	50.0	17.6	0.0	6.3	4.2	11.8	0.0	8.7	7.9	11.5	9.4
WAMPLER	R	VIRGINIA	9	20.0	50.0	26.3	12.5	17.6	16.0	18.8	0.0	13.6	17.9	18.5	18.2
BROYHILL, J	R	VIRGINIA	10	23.5	50.0	28.6	12.5	5.9	8.0	18.8	16.7	18.2	19.5	14.8	17.6
STUBBLEFIEL	D	KENTUCKY	1	47.1	50.0	47.4	50.0	6.3	20.8	40.0	0.0	30.0	45.0	8.7	31.7
NATCHER	D	KENTUCKY	2	47.1	50.0	47.6	50.0	23.5	32.0	41.2	16.7	34.8	45.2	25.9	37.7
COWGER	R	KENTUCKY	3	50.0	50.0	50.0	14.3	16.7	15.8	53.3	0.0	42.1	44.1	20.0	35.2
SNYDER	R	KENTUCKY	4	0.0	0.0	0.0	0.0	7.1	5.6	25.0	0.0	18.2	12.5	4.2	8.9
CARTER	R	KENTUCKY	5	20.0	0.0	16.7	37.5	29.4	32.0	18.8	20.0	19.0	23.1	24.0	23.4
WATTS	D	KENTUCKY	6	31.3	33.3	31.6	66.7	29.4	39.1	43.8	16.7	36.4	42.1	26.9	35.9
PERKINS	D	KENTUCKY	7	82.4	75.0	81.0	62.5	23.5	36.0	70.6	16.7	56.5	73.8	29.6	56.5
MORTON	R	MARYLAND	1	35.3	50.0	38.1	0.0	13.3	10.0	18.8	0.0	14.3	23.7	16.7	21.0
LONG, C.	D	MARYLAND	2	75.0	50.0	70.0	71.4	27.3	44.4	38.5	66.7	47.4	61.1	42.9	54.4
GARMATZ	D	MARYLAND	3	82.4	75.0	81.0	50.0	7.7	23.8	52.9	16.7	43.5	64.3	21.7	49.2
FALLON	D	MARYLAND	4	75.0	66.7	73.7	75.0	8.3	35.0	68.8	20.0	57.1	72.5	20.0	55.0
HOGAN	R	MARYLAND	5				25.0	18.8	20.8	43.8	16.7	36.4	37.5	18.2	28.3
BEALL	R	MARYLAND	6				37.5	17.6	24.0	41.2	16.7	34.8	40.0	17.4	29.2
FREIDEL	D	MARYLAND	7	94.1	75.0	90.5	75.0	35.3	48.0	88.2	66.7	82.6	88.1	48.1	72.5
GUDE	R	MARYLAND	8	100.0	75.0	95.2	66.7	52.9	56.5	75.0	100.0	81.8	84.6	66.7	77.3
BELCHER	R	OKLAHOMA	1	12.5	0.0	10.0	12.5	6.3	8.3	17.6	16.7	17.4	14.6	7.7	11.9
EDMONDSON	D	OKLAHOMA	2	52.9	75.0	57.1	50.0	7.7	23.8	33.3	20.0	30.0	45.0	22.7	37.1
ALBERT	D	OKLAHOMA	3	76.5	75.0	76.2	57.1	18.8	30.4	64.7	16.7	52.2	68.3	26.9	52.2
STEED	D	OKLAHOMA	4	35.3	25.0	33.3	50.0	6.7	21.7	56.3	20.0	47.6	46.3	12.5	33.8
JARMAN	D	OKLAHOMA	5	7.7	0.0	5.9	0.0	7.1	4.5	14.3	16.7	15.0	8.6	8.3	8.5
CAMP	R	OKLAHOMA	6				12.5	7.1	9.1	25.0	16.7	22.7	20.8	10.0	15.9

QUILLEN	R	TENNESSEE	1	18.8	0.0	15.0	12.5	7.1	9.1	11.8	0.0	8.7	14.6	4.2	10.8
DUNCAN	R	TENNESSEE	2	17.6	0.0	14.3	12.5	11.8	12.0	47.1	0.0	34.8	28.6	7.4	20.3
BROCK	R	TENNESSEE	3	12.5	0.0	10.0	0.0	45.5	29.4	12.5	16.7	13.6	10.5	28.6	16.9
EVINS	D	TENNESSEE	4	20.0	100.0	38.5	60.0	7.7	22.2	40.0	16.7	33.3	36.7	22.7	30.8
FULTON, R.	D	TENNESSEE	5	76.9	75.0	76.5	80.0	12.5	38.5	64.3	60.0	63.2	71.9	41.2	61.2
ANDERSON, W	D	TENNESSEE	6	54.5	75.0	60.0	60.0	23.1	33.3	44.4	16.7	33.3	52.0	30.4	41.7
BLANTON	D	TENNESSEE	7	41.7	75.0	50.0	37.5	13.3	21.7	18.2	16.7	17.6	32.3	24.0	28.6
JONES	D	TENNESSEE	8				50.0	12.5	31.3	16.7	0.0	11.8	30.0	7.7	21.2
KUYKENDALL	R	TENNESSEE	9	18.8	0.0	15.0	0.0	0.0	0.0	25.0	0.0	18.2	17.5	0.0	11.9
MOLLOHAN	D	WEST VIRGINIA	1				62.5	7.1	27.3	80.0	0.0	66.7	72.2	6.3	41.2
STAGGERS	D	WEST VIRGINIA	2	85.7	100.0	88.2	57.1	25.0	36.8	64.7	20.0	54.5	71.1	35.0	58.6
SLACK	D	WEST VIRGINIA	3	52.9	100.0	60.0	50.0	12.5	25.0	41.2	0.0	30.4	47.6	20.0	37.3
HECHLER	D	WEST VIRGINIA	4	94.1	75.0	90.5	100.0	94.1	96.0	82.4	100.0	87.0	90.5	92.6	91.3
KEE	D	WEST VIRGINIA	5	69.2	100.0	75.0	50.0	5.9	20.0	47.1	33.3	45.0	55.3	21.7	42.6
RHODES, J.	R	ARIZONA	1	18.8	0.0	15.0	0.0	13.3	8.7	23.5	0.0	18.2	17.1	8.3	13.8
UDALL	D	ARIZONA	2	100.0	75.0	94.4	75.0	58.8	64.0	85.7	50.0	75.0	88.9	59.3	76.2
STEIGER, S.	R	ARIZONA	3	20.0	0.0	15.8	0.0	5.9	4.0	6.3	0.0	4.5	10.3	3.7	7.6
ROGERS, B.	D	COLORADO	1	80.0	75.0	78.9	62.5	31.3	41.7	70.6	66.7	69.6	72.5	46.2	62.1
BROTZMAN	R	COLORADO	2	47.1	33.3	45.0	25.0	12.5	16.7	47.1	16.7	39.1	42.9	16.0	32.8
EVANS	D	COLORADO	3	92.9	75.0	88.9	50.0	64.7	60.0	76.5	66.7	73.9	76.9	66.7	72.7
ASPINALL	D	COLORADO	4	53.3	75.0	57.9	37.5	25.0	30.0	60.0	20.0	50.0	52.6	33.3	45.8
MCCLURE	R	IDAHO	1	17.6	50.0	23.8	16.7	14.3	15.0	17.6	0.0	13.0	17.5	16.7	17.2
HANSEN	R	IDAHO	2	0.0	0.0	0.0	37.5	17.6	24.0	46.2	16.7	36.8	42.9	17.4	29.5
OLSEN	D	MONTANA	1	100.0	100.0	100.0	75.0	47.1	56.0	76.5	100.0	82.6	83.8	64.0	75.8
MELCHER	D	MONTANA	2				80.0	37.5	47.6	75.0	50.0	68.2	76.2	40.9	58.1

Name	Party	State	No.													
BARING	D	NEVADA	0	25.0	0.0	20.0		12.5	7.1	9.1	33.3	0.0	23.5	25.0	4.3	16.9
LUJAN	R	NEW MEXICO	1	25.0	0.0			25.0	13.3	17.4	43.8	60.0	47.6	37.5	25.0	31.8
FOREMAN	R	NEW MEXICO	2	12.5				12.5	5.9	8.0	11.8	0.0	8.7	12.0	4.3	8.3
BURTON, L.	R	UTAH	1	25.0	25.0	25.0		25.0	33.3	30.0	43.8	0.0	31.8	32.5	22.7	29.0
LLOYD	R	UTAH	2	29.4	50.0	33.3		12.5	13.3	13.0	46.7	16.7	38.1	32.5	20.0	27.7
WOLD	R	WYOMING	0					12.5	7.1	9.1	17.6	20.0	18.2	16.0	10.5	13.6
CLAUSEN	R	CALIFORNIA	1	41.2	0.0	33.3		28.6	11.8	16.7	23.5	16.7	21.7	31.7	11.1	23.5
JOHNSON, H.	D	CALIFORNIA	2	88.2	75.0	85.7		62.5	29.4	40.0	70.6	16.7	56.5	76.2	33.3	59.4
MOSS	D	CALIFORNIA	3	100.0	66.7	94.1		75.0	75.0	75.0	83.3	66.7	77.8	88.2	71.4	81.8
LEGGETT	D	CALIFORNIA	4	92.3	75.0	88.2		100.0	61.5	75.0	100.0	66.7	90.0	97.1	65.2	84.2
BURTON, P.	D	CALIFORNIA	5	100.0	100.0	100.0		100.0	86.7	91.3	100.0	100.0	100.0	100.0	91.7	96.8
MAILLIARD	R	CALIFORNIA	6	58.8	66.7	60.0		57.1	15.4	30.0	46.7	16.7	38.1	53.8	22.7	42.6
COHELAN	D	CALIFORNIA	7	100.0	100.0	100.0		100.0	84.6	90.5	100.0	100.0	100.0	100.0	91.3	96.9
MILLER, G.	D	CALIFORNIA	8	93.8	75.0	90.0		62.5	11.8	28.0	75.0	20.0	61.9	80.0	23.1	57.6
EDWARDS, D. D.	D	CALIFORNIA	9	100.0	100.0	100.0		100.0	100.0	100.0	100.0	100.0	100.0	100.0	100.0	100.0
GUBSER	R	CALIFORNIA	10	31.3	33.3	31.6		12.5	6.7	8.7	35.7	16.7	30.0	28.9	12.5	22.6
MCCLOSKEY	R	CALIFORNIA	11	68.8	33.3	63.2		50.0	46.7	47.8	53.3	66.7	57.1	59.0	50.0	55.6
TALCOTT	R	CALIFORNIA	12	37.5	0.0	30.0		25.0	16.7	20.0	23.5	33.3	26.1	29.3	18.2	25.4
TEAGUE, C.	R	CALIFORNIA	13	7.7	0.0	5.9		12.5	7.7	9.5	28.6	0.0	20.0	14.3	5.0	10.4
WALDIE	D	CALIFORNIA	14	100.0	75.0	94.1		100.0	80.0	87.0	94.1	100.0	95.7	97.4	84.0	92.1
MCFALL	D	CALIFORNIA	15	88.2	75.0	85.7		62.5	29.4	40.0	58.8	16.7	47.8	71.4	33.3	56.5
SISK	D	CALIFORNIA	16	86.7	75.0	84.2		50.0	11.8	24.0	68.8	33.3	59.1	71.8	25.9	53.0
ANDERSON	D	CALIFORNIA	17					87.5	52.9	64.0	81.3	66.7	77.3	83.3	56.5	70.2
MATHIAS, R.	R	CALIFORNIA	18	30.8	33.3	31.3		33.3	16.7	25.0	31.3	20.0	28.6	31.4	21.4	28.6
HOLIFIELD	D	CALIFORNIA	19	93.8	100.0	94.4		75.0	30.0	50.0	86.7	16.7	66.7	87.2	33.3	70.2

Name	Party	State	Dist.	1	2	3	4	5	6	7	8	9	10	11	12
SMITH, H.	R	CALIFORNIA	20	14.7	11.5	16.7	21.7	0.0	29.4	12.5	18.8	0.0	9.5	11.8	0.0
HAWKINS	D	CALIFORNIA	21	96.4	100.0	94.3	88.2	100.0	84.6	100.0	100.0	100.0	100.0	100.0	100.0
CORMAN	D	CALIFORNIA	22	79.7	56.5	92.7	77.3	60.0	82.4	70.8	56.3	100.0	94.4	100.0	50.0
CLAWSON	R	CALIFORNIA	23	9.7	9.5	9.8	13.6	0.0	18.8	10.0	16.7	0.0	5.0	5.9	0.0
WIGGINS	R	CALIFORNIA	25	20.3	24.0	17.9	18.2	16.7	18.8	13.0	20.0	0.0	31.6	26.7	50.0
REES	D	CALIFORNIA	26	100.0	100.0	100.0	100.0	100.0	100.0	100.0	100.0	100.0	100.0	100.0	100.0
GOLDWATER	R	CALIFORNIA	27	13.9	11.1	16.7	21.1	16.7	23.1	5.9	8.3	0.0			
BELL	R	CALIFORNIA	28	47.2	26.3	58.8	31.8	16.7	37.5	23.1	22.2	25.0	83.3	92.9	50.0
BROWN, G.	D	CALIFORNIA	29	97.8	100.0	96.8	93.3	100.0	90.9	100.0	100.0	100.0	100.0	100.0	100.0
ROYBAL	D	CALIFORNIA	30	98.5	95.7	100.0	100.0	100.0	100.0	100.0	100.0	100.0	95.2	100.0	75.0
WILSON, C.	D	CALIFORNIA	31	71.7	37.5	94.4	70.6	33.3	90.9	52.2	26.7	100.0	95.0	94.1	100.0
HOSMER	R	CALIFORNIA	32	20.7	5.9	26.8	26.1	16.7	29.4	7.1	0.0	14.3	23.8	29.4	0.0
PETTIS	R	CALIFORNIA	33	28.6	18.5	36.1	35.3	16.7	45.5	16.0	11.8	25.0	38.1	35.3	50.0
HANNA	D	CALIFORNIA	34	67.9	47.1	76.9	61.9	40.0	68.8	52.9	44.4	62.5	88.9	93.3	66.7
WILSON, B.	R	CALIFORNIA	36	17.7	17.4	17.9	23.8	20.0	25.0	9.1	7.1	12.5	21.1	13.3	50.0
VAN DEERLIN	D	CALIFORNIA	37	74.2	59.3	85.7	77.3	66.7	81.3	59.1	52.9	80.0	88.9	92.9	75.0
TUNNEY	D	CALIFORNIA	38	83.7	69.2	90.0	85.7	50.0	100.0	80.0	71.4	87.5	85.7	88.2	75.0
WYATT	R	OREGON	1	40.0	23.1	52.9	27.8	33.3	25.0	34.8	17.6	83.3	57.9	62.5	33.3
ULLMAN	D	OREGON	2	52.4	56.0	50.0	50.0	100.0	35.3	45.5	43.8	50.0	63.2	66.7	50.0
GREEN, E.	D	OREGON	3	42.4	27.8	48.8	40.9	40.0	41.2	25.0	16.7	37.5	64.7	62.5	100.0
DELLENBACK	R	OREGON	4	43.3	30.8	51.2	31.8	16.7	37.5	37.5	31.3	50.0	61.9	64.7	50.0
PELLY	R	WASHINGTON	1	34.4	19.0	42.5	30.0	20.0	33.3	20.0	8.3	37.5	52.4	52.9	50.0
MEEDS	D	WASHINGTON	2	79.0	66.7	86.8	76.2	66.7	80.0	75.0	64.3	100.0	85.7	88.2	75.0
HANSEN, J.	D	WASHINGTON	3	77.6	58.8	85.4	75.0	75.0	75.0	66.7	50.0	87.5	90.0	94.1	66.7
MAY	R	WASHINGTON	4	22.4	19.0	24.3	26.1	16.7	29.4	11.1	9.1	14.3	29.4	23.1	50.0

Name	Party	State													
FOLEY	D	WASHINGTON	5	94.1	75.0	90.5	87.5	52.9	64.0	76.5	80.0	77.3	85.7	61.5	76.5
HICKS	D	WASHINGTON	6	88.2	75.0	85.7	87.5	42.9	59.1	58.8	66.7	60.9	76.2	54.2	68.2
ADAMS	D	WASHINGTON	7	100.0	75.0	95.2	87.5	60.0	69.6	87.5	100.0	90.9	92.7	72.0	84.8
POLLOCK	R	ALASKA	0	53.3	66.7	55.6	50.0	0.0	21.4	45.5	0.0	41.7	50.0	16.7	40.9
MATSUNAGA	D	HAWAII	0	100.0	100.0	100.0	87.5	41.2	56.0	94.1	66.7	87.0	95.0	55.6	79.1
MINK	D	HAWAII	0	94.1	100.0	95.2	100.0	70.6	80.0	94.1	50.0	82.6	95.2	70.4	85.5
DODD	D	CONNECTICUT	0	75.0	0.0	42.9	58.7	13.0	43.5	61.1	0.0	50.0	63.1	7.1	44.4
RIBICOFF	D	CONNECTICUT	0	100.0	41.7	78.8	93.6	82.6	90.0	92.3	94.4	92.9	94.2	77.4	89.0
MUSKIE	D	MAINE	0	94.4	30.8	67.7	84.1	77.3	81.8	98.0	100.0	98.5	92.0	72.5	86.0
SMITH	R	MAINE	0	54.5	26.7	43.2	28.6	34.8	30.6	51.0	50.0	50.7	42.6	37.5	41.0
KENNEDY, E. D		MASSACHUSETTS	0	100.0	100.0	100.0	97.7	95.2	96.9	100.0	81.3	94.8	99.0	90.9	96.6
BROOKE	R	MASSACHUSETTS	0	95.5	53.3	78.4	83.7	69.6	79.2	92.3	88.9	91.4	89.4	71.4	83.8
COTTON	R	NEW HAMPSHIRE	0	55.6	10.0	39.3	10.6	17.4	12.9	30.6	5.9	24.2	26.3	12.0	22.0
MCINTYRE	D	NEW HAMPSHIRE	0	81.8	20.0	56.8	76.1	52.2	68.1	78.3	61.1	73.4	78.1	46.4	67.6
PASTORE	D	RHODE ISLAND	0	86.4	26.7	62.2	81.6	47.8	70.8	92.3	83.3	90.0	87.0	53.6	76.5
PELL	D	RHODE ISLAND	0	95.5	71.4	86.1	89.1	87.0	88.4	93.8	88.9	92.4	92.2	83.6	89.5
AIKEN	R	VERMONT	0	66.7	30.8	51.6	46.9	63.6	52.1	62.5	77.8	66.7	56.5	60.4	57.7
PROUTY	R	VERMONT	0	68.4	30.8	53.1	46.8	60.0	50.7	77.8	27.8	63.5	63.1	41.2	56.2
BOGGS	R	DELAWARE	0	63.6	20.0	45.9	31.9	33.3	32.4	65.4	16.7	52.9	52.1	24.1	43.4
WILLIAMS, J R	R	DELAWARE	0	4.5	40.0	18.9	21.7	28.6	23.9	26.9	27.8	27.1	20.8	31.5	24.1
CASE	R	NEW JERSEY	0	100.0	60.0	87.5	84.4	85.7	84.8	94.2	88.9	92.9	91.6	81.6	88.7
WILLIAMS, H D	D	NEW JERSEY	0	100.0	71.4	88.9	93.3	91.3	92.6	93.8	88.9	92.4	94.8	85.5	91.8
GOODELL	R	NEW YORK	0	100.0	50.0	66.7	89.1	95.7	91.3	100.0	83.3	95.7	94.9	88.4	92.9
JAVITS	R	NEW YORK	0	100.0	64.3	86.1	82.6	87.0	84.1	97.9	94.4	97.0	92.2	83.6	89.5
SCOTT	R	PENNSYLVANIA	0	95.5	20.0	64.9	51.0	30.4	44.4	76.9	18.8	63.2	69.9	24.1	55.9

NAME	P	STATE	D	1968			1969			1970			TOTAL		
				DOM	DEF	TOT	DOM	DEF	TOT	DOM	DEF	TOT	DOM	DEF	TOT
SCHWEIKER	R	PENNSYLVANIA	0				68.8	82.6	73.2	86.5	83.3	85.7	78.0	82.9	79.4
PERCY	R	ILLINOIS	0	100.0	46.7	78.4	60.0	63.6	61.2	82.4	38.9	71.0	77.1	50.9	68.8
SMITH	R	ILLINOIS	0				35.3	27.3	33.3	42.0	22.2	36.8	39.3	24.1	35.4
HARTKE	D	INDIANA	0	85.7	81.8	84.4	90.7	90.0	90.5	89.2	81.3	86.8	89.1	85.1	87.8
BAYH	D	INDIANA	0	89.5	45.5	73.3	90.9	89.5	90.5	97.4	76.5	90.9	93.1	74.5	87.2
GRIFFIN	R	MICHIGAN	0	85.7	7.1	54.3	44.2	26.1	37.9	67.4	16.7	52.5	61.7	18.2	46.9
HART	D	MICHIGAN	0	100.0	86.7	94.6	93.9	95.7	94.4	100.0	88.9	97.1	97.6	91.1	95.5
YOUNG, S.	D	OHIO	0	95.5	93.3	94.6	84.4	85.7	84.8	97.4	88.9	94.6	91.4	90.9	90.6
SAXBE	R	OHIO	0				42.1	90.9	60.0	72.0	70.6	71.4	54.0	82.1	64.7
PROXMIRE	D	WISCONSIN	0	86.4	93.3	89.2	69.4	95.7	77.8	84.6	94.4	87.1	78.9	94.6	83.8
NELSON	D	WISCONSIN	0	95.5	100.0	97.1	100.0	91.3	97.0	97.9	93.8	96.9	98.2	94.2	97.0
MILLER	R	IOWA	0	22.7	6.7	16.2	18.4	21.7	19.4	40.4	11.1	32.9	28.5	14.3	24.0
HUGHES	D	IOWA	0				91.1	95.7	92.6	95.7	100.0	96.9	93.4	97.6	94.7
DOLE	R	KANSAS	0				14.6	13.6	14.3	44.9	27.8	40.3	29.9	20.0	27.0
PEARSON	R	KANSAS	0	59.1	0.0	36.1	24.4	57.1	34.8	70.8	16.7	56.1	50.4	28.3	43.5
MCCARTHY	D	MINNESOTA	0	100.0	100.0	100.0	79.4	86.7	81.6	100.0	87.5	93.9	88.1	87.9	88.0
MONDALE	D	MINNESOTA	0	100.0	83.3	93.5	97.4	100.0	98.4	100.0	94.1	98.5	99.1	94.2	97.5
SYMINGTON	D	MISSOURI	0	72.7	64.3	69.4	66.7	57.1	63.8	89.8	72.2	85.1	78.8	65.2	74.7
EAGLETON	D	MISSOURI	0				83.3	95.7	87.7	90.4	94.1	91.3	87.2	95.0	89.6
CURTIS	R	NEBRASKA	0	13.6	0.0	8.1	4.1	0.0	2.8	2.0	11.1	4.3	4.9	3.6	4.5
HRUSKA	R	NEBRASKA	0	14.3	6.7	11.1	4.2	8.7	5.6	7.8	11.1	8.7	7.5	8.9	8.0
BURDICK	D	NORTH DAKOTA	0	90.5	46.2	73.5	54.4	69.6	66.2	87.5	88.9	87.9	78.9	70.4	76.2
YOUNG, M.	R	NORTH DAKOTA	0	13.6	7.1	11.1	16.3	13.6	15.5	23.4	5.6	18.5	18.6	9.3	15.7
MCGOVERN	D	SOUTH DAKOTA	0	88.9	100.0	93.5	95.7	90.9	94.2	100.0	100.0	100.0	96.4	96.2	96.3

Name	Party	State													
MUNDT	R	SOUTH DAKOTA	0	9.5	7.1	8.6	4.3	7.1	5.4	16.3	11.1	14.8	11.5	8.7	10.5
SPARKMAN	D	ALABAMA	0	9.5	7.1	8.6	17.5	34.8	23.8	7.7	17.6	10.1	11.5	22.2	15.0
ALLEN	D	ALABAMA	0				14.9	17.4	15.7	6.1	11.1	7.5	10.4	14.6	11.7
FULBRIGHT	D	ARKANSAS	0	21.4	71.4	38.1	60.9	86.4	69.1	38.6	88.9	53.2	46.2	85.1	58.3
MCCLELLAN	D	ARKANSAS	0	0.0	0.0	0.0	10.0	9.1	9.7	4.8	6.7	5.3	5.9	5.9	5.9
HOLLAND	D	FLORIDA	0	0.0	6.7	2.7	8.2	8.7	8.3	1.9	16.7	5.7	4.1	10.7	6.1
GURNEY	R	FLORIDA	0	0.0	0.0	0.0	2.2	8.7	4.3	5.0	11.1	6.9	3.5	9.8	5.5
TALMADGE	D	GEORGIA	0	11.8	7.1	9.7	15.6	5.0	12.3	4.5	16.7	6.0	10.4	7.5	9.6
RUSSELL	D	GEORGIA	0	0.0	0.0	0.0	12.8	0.0	9.1	17.0	11.8	15.6	12.4	4.2	9.8
ELLENDER	D	LOUISIANA	0	9.1	20.0	13.5	16.3	47.8	26.4	3.8	41.2	13.0	9.8	38.2	18.5
LONG, R.	D	LOUISIANA	0	10.0	0.0	6.3	12.5	5.9	10.5	11.1	25.0	14.8	11.4	11.1	11.3
EASTLAND	D	MISSISSIPPI	0	0.0	0.0	0.0	12.5	0.0	7.7	12.5	22.2	15.2	9.8	8.0	9.2
STENNIS	D	MISSISSIPPI	0	4.8	0.0	2.9	12.8	4.3	10.0	6.4	11.1	7.7	8.7	5.5	7.6
ERVIN	D	NORTH CAROLINA	0	4.8	7.1	5.7	13.0	0.0	8.7	1.9	11.1	4.3	6.7	5.5	6.3
JORDAN, B.	D	NORTH CAROLINA	0	5.3	0.0	3.3	15.9	4.5	12.1	5.9	50.0	17.4	9.6	19.6	12.7
THURMOND	R	SOUTH CAROLINA	0	0.0	0.0	0.0	2.1	8.7	4.2	3.8	5.6	4.3	2.5	5.4	3.4
HOLLINGS	D	SOUTH CAROLINA	0	10.5	7.7	9.4	35.1	11.8	27.8	28.3	38.9	31.3	27.5	20.8	25.3
YARBOROUGH	D	TEXAS	0	77.8	41.7	63.3	70.5	85.0	75.0	81.3	100.0	86.4	75.5	77.3	76.1
TOWER	R	TEXAS	0	4.5	6.7	5.4	2.1	13.6	5.7	3.8	5.6	4.3	3.3	9.1	5.1
BYRD, H.	D	VIRGINIA	0	4.5	20.0	10.8	8.3	27.3	14.3	7.7	27.8	12.9	7.4	25.5	13.0
SPONG	D	VIRGINIA	0	27.3	20.0	24.3	38.8	43.5	40.3	36.5	55.6	41.4	35.8	41.1	37.4
COOPER	R	KENTUCKY	0	68.2	64.3	66.7	52.9	73.7	60.4	62.7	77.8	66.7	60.7	72.5	64.6
COOK	R	KENTUCKY	0				48.9	65.0	53.8	71.4	12.5	56.9	60.6	41.7	55.4
MATHIAS	R	MARYLAND	0				72.7	81.8	75.8	88.6	82.4	86.9	80.7	82.1	81.1
TYDINGS	D	MARYLAND	0	100.0	86.7	94.4	88.1	83.3	86.7	94.9	87.5	92.7	93.1	85.7	90.7

Name	Party	State													
HARRIS	D	OKLAHOMA	85.4	73.3	90.2	96.9	88.2	100.0	80.0	90.0	75.6	71.4	0.0	100.0	0
BELLMON	R	OKLAHOMA	32.1	21.1	36.4	40.3	11.8	50.0	24.3	28.6	22.4	48.3	44.4	50.0	0
GORE	D	TENNESSEE	65.2	73.8	63.3	71.2	85.7	66.7	69.8	78.9	65.9	48.3		50.0	0
BAKER	R	TENNESSEE	25.7	14.9	30.7	24.6	11.1	30.8	24.2	25.0	23.8	31.0	0.0	45.0	0
BYRD, R.	D	WEST VIRGINIA	32.2	38.2	29.5	40.0	50.0	36.5	32.9	40.9	29.2	16.2	20.0	13.6	0
RANDOLPH	D	WEST VIRGINIA	64.2	66.1	63.4	70.0	77.8	67.3	59.7	65.2	57.1	62.2	53.3	68.2	0
GOLDWATER	R	ARIZONA	12.2	8.1	14.8	23.4	11.8	30.0	2.0	5.0	0.0	8.1			0
FANNIN	R	ARIZONA	7.6	5.4	8.7	11.3	5.6	13.6	4.2	8.7	2.0	8.1	0.0	13.6	0
ALLOTT	R	COLORADO	19.9	10.7	24.2	25.7	11.1	30.8	9.7	17.4	6.1	29.4	0.0	52.6	0
DOMINICK	R	COLORADO	28.5	11.1	36.9	40.0	11.1	52.4	14.3	19.0	12.2	37.1	0.0	65.0	0
CHURCH	D	IDAHO	83.2	89.6	80.0	90.7	88.9	91.7	81.5	91.3	76.2	70.8	85.7	64.7	0
JORDAN, L.	R	IDAHO	31.9	21.8	36.9	38.1	16.7	46.7	28.8	31.8	27.3	27.0	13.3	36.4	0
MANSFIELD	D	MONTANA	72.8	77.8	70.4	83.8	88.9	82.0	66.7	78.3	60.9	62.5	61.5	63.2	0
METCALF	D	MONTANA	81.4	76.9	83.9	91.3	87.5	93.3	69.2	66.7	70.5	91.2	80.0	100.0	0
BIBLE	D	NEVADA	30.0	18.8	34.8	39.4	29.4	42.9	25.4	14.3	30.4	18.5	10.0	23.5	0
CANNON	D	NEVADA	39.5	17.0	50.0	50.0	25.0	57.7	35.4	22.7	41.9	26.5	0.0	47.4	0
ANDERSON	D	NEW MEXICO	50.8	30.2	61.4	65.0	50.0	71.4	40.0	30.8	45.5	35.5	0.0	57.9	0
MONTOYA	D	NEW MEXICO	69.6	49.0	79.1	85.9	77.8	89.1	58.5	36.4	69.8	59.4	27.3	76.2	0
BENNETT	R	UTAH	9.8	13.0	8.3	11.8	11.1	12.0	10.1	23.8	4.2	5.4	0.0	9.1	0
MOSS	D	UTAH	82.2	78.2	84.3	86.9	82.4	88.6	80.0	82.6	78.6	78.4	66.7	86.4	0
MCGEE	D	WYOMING	64.9	22.2	85.1	76.5	22.2	96.0	52.3	22.7	67.4	65.7	21.4	95.2	0
HANSEN	R	WYOMING	12.1	9.6	13.1	17.4	5.6	21.6	6.9	13.0	4.1	12.1	9.1	13.6	0
MURPHY	R	CALIFORNIA	14.9	7.4	18.4	20.6	11.1	24.4	8.8	9.5	8.5	16.2	0.0	27.3	0
CRANSTON	D	CALIFORNIA	88.1	85.4	89.2	89.6	83.3	91.8	86.6	87.0	86.4				0
HATFIELD	R	OREGON	86.3	89.1	85.0	92.5	94.1	92.0	77.5	91.3	70.8	91.9	80.0	100.0	0

PACKWOOD	R	OREGON	0				55.6	65.2	58.8	76.9	46.7	68.5	65.5	57.9	63.1
JACKSON	D	WASHINGTON	0	86.4	0.0	51.4	85.7	30.4	68.1	86.5	38.9	74.3	86.2	25.0	67.0
MAGNUSON	D	WASHINGTON	0	80.0	0.0	45.7	69.4	59.1	66.2	84.0	83.3	83.8	77.3	50.9	69.0
GRAVEL	D	ALASKA	0				68.3	88.9	74.6	65.0	83.3	70.7	66.7	86.1	72.6
STEVENS	R	ALASKA	0	72.2	0.0	39.4	32.5	20.0	28.3	58.6	26.7	47.7	43.5	22.9	36.5
FONG	R	HAWAII	0				50.0	21.7	40.3	70.6	16.7	56.5	62.8	14.3	46.7
INOUYE	D	HAWAII	0	100.0	38.5	73.3	78.0	71.4	76.4	95.2	93.8	94.8	89.0	69.8	83.2

79

C. REGISTRATION LAWS IN THE FIFTY STATES

United States citizenship is a requirement for voting in all states. Minimum legal voting age is 21 in all states except Hawaii (20), Georgia and Kentucky (18), and Alaska, Maryland, and possibly Nebraska (19). Most states require registration in advance of voting.

The following notes apply to columns a-e of the tables that follow them.

(a) In many states it is possible to register by mail rather than in person. To do so, write to the voter registration office listed and request an "Affidavit of Registration" or other register-by-mail form as your state requires.

(b) There is a residence requirement in most states, counties, and precincts in order to become a registered voter (y = years, m = months, and d = days).

(c) If you have registered previously, you won't have to again providing you have not changed your name or address (legal residence) and:

1 - have voted in last year's general election
2 - have voted at least once in the past two calendar years
3 - "   "   "   "   "   "   "   "   three years
4 - "   "   "   "   "   "   "   "   four years
5 - "   "   "   "   "   "   "   "   five years
p - your voting record doesn't matter (permanent registration)
Ann. - all voters must reregister every year (annual registration)
Dec. - all voters must reregister once every 10 years (decennial registration).

(d) As noted, a few states have two primaries. (The second is usually for run-offs.) Some states have none; they nominate candidates by party convention or party committee. In several states parties endorse candidates by convention but actually nominate by primary. Check with your local government, party office, or League of Women Voters for more details.

(e) Most states allow qualified voters who are studying away from home to vote by absentee ballot. Some states have particular forms for application for an absentee ballot. Leave plenty of time to request, complete, and return such forms.

(1) Only pre-voting in person from the 20th to 5th day before the election.

(2) with Registrar of Voters in L.A., S.F., San Diego, San Bernardino and Santa Clara counties.

(3) with the Election Commissioner in Denver.

(4) with the Bd. of Election Commissioners in Chicago Election District.

(5) For Chicago, Chicago Heights, Berwyn, Cicero, Stickney, and Lyons, write Chicago Bd. of Elections, City Hall Room 308. For rest of Cook County write County Clerk, Election Dept., Room 230, Cook County Building, Chicago.

(con't on page 83)

State	Last Day to Register (1970)	By Mail?	Where to Register (a)	State	County	Precint
ALA.	10/21	N	County Board of Registrars	1y	6m	3m
ALASKA	10/19	Y		1y		30d
ARIZ	9/21	Y	County Recorder	1y	30d	30d
ARK	10/14	Y	Permanent Registrar or Deputy	1y	6m	30d
CALIF	9/10	Y	County Clerk (2)	1y	90d	54d
COLO	10/14	Y	County Clerk (3)	1y	90d	20d
CONN	10/10	N	Town Clerk		6m	
DEL	10/17	N	Cty. Dept. of Elections	1y	90d	30d
FLA		N	Cty. Super. of Registration	1y	6m	
GA	9/14	N	Cty. Bd. of Registrars	1y	6m	
HA	10/13	Y	County Clerk (Hon.=City Clerk)	1y	3m	3m
IDAHO	10/31	Y	Cty. Auditor or Recorder	6m	30d	
ILL	10/5	Y	County Clerk (4)	1y	90d	30d
IND	10/5	N	Cty. Clerk or Bd. of Regis.	6m	60d	30d
IOWA	10/24	N	City or Twn. Clerk	6m	60d	30d
KANS	10/13	Y	City Clerk (6)	6m		30d
KEN	9/5	N	County Clerk (7)	1y	6m	60d
LA	10/3	N	Registrar of Parish	1y	6m	3m
MAINE	Varies	Y	Bd. of Select. or Regis.	6m	3m	
MD	10/5	Y	Bd. of Super. of Elections	6m	3m	
MASS	10/3	N	City or Town Clerk	1y	6m	
MICH	10/2	N	City or Town Clerk	6m		30d
MINN	10/13	Y	City Clerk or Com. of Regis.	6m		30d
MISS	7/3	Y	City or County Registrar	2y	1y	1y
MO	10/5-10	N	County Clerk (9)	1y	60d	60d
MONT	9/24	Y	Cty. Clerk & Recorder	1y	30d	
NEB	10/23	Y	County Clerk (11)	6m	10d	10d
NEV	9/26	Y	County Clerk	6m	30d	10d
N.H.	10/24-8	Y	Bd. of Supervisors	6m	6m	
N.J.	9/24	N	City Clerk or Com. of Reg.	6m	40d	
N.M.	9/22	Y	County Clerk	1y	90d	30d
N.Y.	Varies	Y	Cty. Bd. of Elections	3m	3m	3m
N.C.	10/24	N	Regis. or Cty. Bd. of Elec.	1y		30d
N.D.	Not req.			1y	90d	30d
OHIO	9/23	N	Cty. Bd. of Elections	1y	40d	40d
OKLA	10/23	N	Cty. Bd. of Elec. or Regis.	6m	2m	20d
ORE	10/3	Y	County Clerk (12)	6m		
PA	9/14	N	Cty. Bd. of Elections (13)	90d		60d
R.I.	9/4	N	Bd. of Canv. & Regis.	1y	6m	
S.C.	10/3	N	Cty. Regis. Board	1y	6m	3m
S.D.	10/14	Y	County Auditor	1y	90d	30d
TENN	10/3	Y	Cty. Regis. at Large	1y	3m	
TEXAS	1/31	Y	Cty. Tax Assessor	1y	6m	
UTAH	10/28	Y	County Clerk	1y	4m	60d
VT	10/31	Y	Bd. of Civil Authority	1y	90d	
VA	10/3	N	General Registrar	1y	6m	30d
WASH	10/3	N	City Clerk, Cty. Auditor	1y	90d	30d
W.VA.	10/3	Y	Clerk of Circuit Court	1y	60d	
WISC	10/14-21	Y	City/Town/Vill. Clerk (14)	6m		10d
WYO	10/19	Y	County Clerk	1y	60d	10d

Gen. Elec.	Prim.	Request Absentee Ballot (e)	Get Absentee Ballot from (e)
(1)	(1)	45–5 days before election	County Registrar in Equity District or Deputy Magis.
Y	Y	6 mo.–4 days b.e.	County Recorder
Y	Y	30 days–last Sat. b.e.	County Clerk
Y	Y	90–0 days b.e.	County Clerk (2)
Y	Y	60–7 days b.e.	County Clerk (3)
Y	Y	90 days–last Fri. b.e.	Town Clerk
Y	N	45–4 days b.e.	Cty. Dept of Elecs.
Y		30–10 days b.e.	Cty. Super. of Elecs.
Y	Y	5–1 days b.e.	Cty. Bd. of Registrars
Y	Y	90–5 days b.e.	County Clerk
Y	Y	60–10 days b.e.	County Auditor or Recorder
Y	Y	Any time	County Clerk (5)
Y	Y	60–30 days b.e.	Ct. Election Board
Y	Y	17 days–last Sat. b.e.	County Auditor, City Clerk
Y	Y	20–0 days b.e.	County Clerk of Elecs.
Y	Y	65 days–12 noon elec. day	Clerk of County Court
Y	Y	Postmark 20+ days b.e.	Clerk of Parish Courty
Y	Y	60–7 days b.e.	Town or City Clerk
Y	Y	Any time	Bd. of Super. of Elecs.
Y	Y	Up to 10 days b.e.	Town or City Clerk
Y	N	Any time	Town or City Clerk
Y	Y	75 days–2 p.m. Sat. b.e.	County Auditor
Y	Y	45–1 days b.e.	City or Cty. Registrar
N	N	60–0 days b.e.	Cty. Clerk or Bd. of Elecs.
Y	Y	30–6 days b.e.	County Clerk
Y	Y	45–1 days b.e.	County Clerk (11)
Y	Y	90–2 days b.e.	County Clerk or Registrar
Y	Y	Till 5 p.m. Tues. b.e.	City or Town Clerk
Y	N	Any time	County Clerk
Y	Y	8 days b.e.	County Clerk
Y	Y	10 days b.e.	Board of Elections
Y	N	30–7 days b.e.	Chm., County Bd. of Elections
Y	N	45–5 days b.e.	County Auditor
Y	Y	30–0 days b.e.	Cler, Cty. Bd. of Elections
Y	Y	30–5 days b.e.	County Board of Elections
Y	Y	Any time, prefer 30 days b.e.	County Clerk (12)
Y	Y	60–5 days b.e.	Chief Clerk, Cty. Bd. Elecs.
Y	Y	7 days b.e.	Local Bd. of Canvassers
Y	Y	21 days b.e.	Bd. of Reg., Cty. of Resid.
Y	Y	Any time	County or City Auditor
Y	Y	Any time	County Election Commission
Y	Y	40–5 days b.e.	County Clerk
Y	Y	60–4 days b.e.	County Clerk
Y	Y	30–0 days b.e.	Town Clerk
Y	Y	Up to 4 days b.e.	Precinct or Gen. Registrar
Y	Y	60–5 days b.e.	County Auditor, City Clerk
Y	Y	45–0 days b.e.	Clerk of Circuit Court
Y	Y	60–3 days b.e.	Town or City Clerk (14)
Y	Y	90–3 days b.e.	County Clerk
Y	Y	40–0 days b.e.	

(6) In Johnson, Sedgwick, Shawnee & Wyandotte counties with Election Commissioners.

(7) Louisville--Board of Registration Commissioners

(8) In St. Louis and Kansas City, and in Clay, Jackson and St. Louis counties--with Board of Election Commissioners,

(9) Douglas and Lancaster counties--Election Commissioner

(10) Multnomah County--Registrar of Elections

(11) Philadelphia--Registration Commission

(12) Milwaukee--Board of Election Commissioners

NOTES TO CHAPTER 1

1. Charles O. Jones, "Interparty Competition for Congressional Seats," Western Political Quarterly (1964), 461-476, has a good discussion of historical trends in Congressional elections.

2. See Raymond Wolfinger and Joan Heifetz, "Safe Seats, Seniority, and Power in Congress," American Political Science Review (1965), 337-349.

3. See Barbara Hinckley, "Interpreting House Midterm Elections," American Political Science Review (1967), 694-700.

4. See Alexander Heard, The Costs of Democracy (1960).

5. Donald Stokes and Warren Miller, "Party Government and the Saliency of Congress," in Angus Campbell, et al., Elections and the Political Order (1967).

6. Stephen Shadegg, How to Win Elections (1965).

7. Stokes and Miller, "Party Government."

NOTES TO CHAPTER 3

1. Anthony Downs, An Economic Theory of Democracy 1956.

2. Stanley Kelley, William Bowen, and Richard Ayres, "Registration and Voting: Putting First Things First," American Political Science Review (1967), 359-379.

3. Morris Rosenberg, "Test Factor Standardization as a Method of Interpretation," Social Forces, 41 (1962), 53-61.

4. G. Allen Brunner and Stephen J. Carroll, "The Effect of Prior Telephone Appointments on Completion Rates and Response Content," Public Opinion Quarterly, 31 (Winter 1967-1968), 652-654.

NOTES TO CHAPTER 4

1. Abraham Lincoln, Illinois State Register, February 21, 1840

2. Gerold Kramer, "The Effects of Precinct-Level Canvassing on Voter Behavior," unpublished manuscript, Yale University, July 15, 1969.

NOTES TO CHAPTER 6

1. Raymond Bauer, Ithiel de Sola Pool, and Lewis Dexter, _American Business and Public Policy_, (1963), contains an excellent discussion of the various aspects of lobbying.

2. Donald R. Matthews, in _U.S. Senators and Their World_ (1960), devotes a chapter to disucssing the Senate folkways.

3. Huitt describes William Proxmire's behavior in his early Senate years in "The Outsider in the Senate: An Alternative Role," in Ralph Huitt and Robert Peabody, _Congress: Two Decades of Analysis_ (1969).

4. Nicholas Masters, "Committee Assignments," in Robert Peabody and Nelson Polsby, _New Perspectives on the House of Representatives_, 2nd edition (1969).

5. Nelson Polsby, "Two Strategies of Influence: Choosing a Majority Leader, 1962," in Peabody and Polsby, _New Perspectives on the House of Representatives_.

6. Now up to 20.

7. Richard Fenno, "The Internal Distribution of Influence: The House," in David Truman, _The Congress and America's Future_ (1965).

MAR 2 9 1984

DISCHARGED 1909

DISCHARGED

DISCHARGED 1984